Nelson Thornes Shakespeare

Much Ado About Nothing

TEACHER RESOURCE BOOK

Volume editor: **Lawrence Green**

Series editors: **Duncan Beal** and **Dinah Jurksaitis**

Series consultant: **Peter Thomas**

Published in 2004 by:
Nelson Thornes Ltd
Delta Place
27 Bath Road
CHELTENHAM
GL53 7TH
United Kingdom

04 05 06 07 08 / 10 9 8 7 6 5 4 3 2 1

A catalogue record for this book is available from the British Library

ISBN 0-7487-8607-4

Illustrations by Angela Lumley
Page make-up by Tech Set

Printed and bound in Croatia by Zrinski

Acknowledgements
www.CartoonStock.com/Kes, p. 2; www.CartoonStock.com/Dean Moore, p. 30; www.CartoonStock.com/Joel Mishon, p. 32; Hulton-Deutsch Collection/Corbis, p. 23; Mary Evans Picture Library, pp. 3, 9, 16, 27.

Contents

Activity grids

Student activities grouped according to subject areas

Subject	Activity Sheet Numbers
Language	1, 2, 3, 6, 9 14, 15, 18, 19, 21, 22, 25, 29, 31, 32
Context	2, 13, 18, 19, 21, 26, 32, 33, 34
Staging	3, 4, 10, 11, 12, 14, 15, 16, 20, 21, 23
Interpretation	5, 7, 12
Structure	7, 8, 10, 11, 15, 17, 18, 20, 24, 27
Specific to character	
Beatrice	1, 11, 19, 22, 35-37
Benedick	1, 11, 22, 38–41
Leonato	3, 6, 42–44
Claudio	6, 21, 45–47
Hero	6, 48–50
Don Pedro	6, 51–52
Don John	4, 34, 53–54
Dogberry	14, 20

Student activities particularly appropriate for suggested coursework assignments

GCSE

Assignment 1	4, 7, 8, 9, 11, 17, 18, 19, 21, 22, 24
Assignment 2	1, 2, 6, 8, 10, 11, 12, 13, 14, 16, 20, 22
Assignment 3	1, 4, 5, 7, 8, 9, 13, 17, 18, 19, 21, 24, 34
Assignment 4	1, 2, 5, 6, 8, 10, 11, 12, 18, 19, 21, 22, 24

AS LEVEL

Assignment 5	1, 2, 5, 7, 10, 11, 14, 16, 17, 18, 19, 21, 22
Assignment 6	2, 4, 5, 6, 9, 10, 11, 12, 18, 19, 21, 23

Introduction

To the teacher

In the **student editions** you will find:

- **introductory essays** concerned with the play's cultural context, or literary sources
- **introductions** to each scene
- **line by line notes** on vocabulary and idiom
- **explanations of interesting points** of language and versification, such as imagery, wordplay, verse and prose
- **performance features** – often one per page – inviting students to consider the play in performance: the possibilities of character presentation, of action, and of mood
- **comparison features** at the end of each scene providing a cross-reference with related scenes and threads. The student's experience of the play is often disjointed, spread over a series of lessons, so this feature helps to see how a scene fits the wider picture
- **scene summaries** at the end of each scene.

In this **Resource Book** you will find challenging activities to complement a reading of the play.

- **Scene by scene worksheets** are designed to help students think about the events of a scene in the context of the whole play. Most worksheets comprise clear tasks, such as a search for evidence to support a view of a character. Some are more explanatory, developing a language point. These sheets are suitable for both writing and discussion. They are particularly useful for helping an absentee student catch up on missed scenes.
- **Character Sheets** allow students to see how our view of a character develops over the course of the play.
- A series of **Coursework Assignments** suggest areas for written or oral responses. The teacher can select one before the class begins to study the play. At the end of each Act students consider how the events of that Act contribute towards that assignment. By the time they have read the play students will have the understanding and reference necessary to respond to a demanding task.
- At least one of the assignment essay titles addresses the play in performance, providing students with an opportunity to consider different social and historical settings and interpretations. This encourages students to see the play not as a historical relic, but to appreciate the way it spans the centuries.

Our aim is to provide a resource for teachers which recognises the problems of school-based Shakespeare: a play written to be performed, but largely experienced as a text to be read in a class; a play often read with specific ends in mind depending on the syllabus followed. We hope that this Resource Book will offer support to the teacher faced with this rewarding challenge.

Duncan Beal and Dinah Jurksaitis

Round one...!

Language and **Character**

We have already witnessed the withering wit of Beatrice which left the Messenger admitting her superiority: **I will hold friends with you, lady** *(line 66)*.

Leonato has also told us of the **merry war** *(line 45)* between Beatrice and Benedick.

When Benedick finally comes on stage, therefore, our expectations have been raised; we anticipate the latest round in their ongoing contest – and we are not disappointed!

The war is one of wit and their weapons are words, the verbal equivalent of a fencing or modern boxing match in which each contestant tries to score points off his opponent before delivering a 'knock-out punch'.

1 Show how Beatrice and Benedick punch, parry and counter-punch in this brief opening sparring match.

Look again at lines 86–107 and see who wins this first round.

2 Summarise briefly in your own words as far as possible each verbal attack that each aims at his or her opponent and award points (between 1 and 3) depending on how effective you think the point is. Be prepared to justify your allocation of points. Here are a couple of examples to start you off:

Beatrice	Score	Benedick	Score
1 Beatrice wonders why Benedick keeps talking since no one is listening to him.	2	1	☐
2		2 (a) Benedick mocks her with the name *Lady Disdain*.	1
		(b) He pretends astonishment that she is still alive.	☐
	☐		
3 (a) Scorn can never die while Benedick is alive to provide it with food.	☐	3	☐
(b) Benedick's very presence is enough to change Good Manners into Scorn.	☐		☐
TOTAL		**TOTAL**	

Comrades-in-arms

Character and Language

Don Pedro, Benedick and Claudio have clearly developed a strong bond of male (possibly 'macho'?) comradeship during the recent military campaign and this bond continues in civilian surroundings.

- Look carefully at the conversation between Claudio and Benedick (lines 119–49). Claudio is obviously seriously in love with everything about Hero; Benedick is teasing him unmercifully by suggesting that she is 'nothing special'. Make a note of each of the 'put-downs' that Benedick uses and show how it is effective.

The cuckold has always been a figure of ridicule.

Praise	Put-down
Claudio 'noted' Hero, i.e. he has observed her closely.	Benedick has 'looked on her', i.e. but she wasn't worth 'noting'.

As with most groups of young men today, the conversation eventually turns to the subjects of sport (i.e. war) and women (i.e. sex). These men, however, are also courtiers. They pride themselves on their education and will use their learning as weapons in this friendly war of words.

Language

Look carefully at the conversation between the three young men in this scene (lines 150–249). Make a note of the subjects and issues that they draw on in their conversation, quote brief examples of each and say how each reference is used. Create a table like this one:

Subject	Example	How used
Honour/loyalty	**I charge thee on thy allegiance** *(line 153)*	Don Pedro 'forces' Benedick to tell him the gossip by pulling rank as his Prince.
Sex		
Marriage		
Religion		

Great preparation

Leonato is a wealthy man and he holds high office as Governor of Messina. However, he is not of noble rank like the Prince, Don Pedro or Count Claudio. An extended visit from the Prince to his house would be a great honour as well as a personal pleasure and he is clearly anxious to impress.

He goes to a great deal of trouble to entertain Don Pedro and his other high-born guests in a manner befitting their rank and his own sense of wealth and status. Don Pedro realises that **indeed he hath made great preparation** *(Act 1 Scene 1, line 202)*.

Leonato's 'great preparation' includes a group of musicians.

Character

1   Look back at Scene 1. Find evidence that Leonato's wealth is of significant interest to at least one of the characters:

_____

_____

2   Leonato is anxious to fulfil his role as genial and hospitable host. How would you describe the way he behaves towards his high-born guests: deferential, flattering, awkward, over-anxious to please, polite but not over-awed? Note down brief quotations to support your views:

_____

_____

Staging and Language

In the short Act 1 Scene 2 we see Leonato's **great preparation** in progress. It is a bustling and lively scene.

- How does Shakespeare create this sense of urgency and frantic activity in his sentence structure? Look, for example, at sentence length and type.

- Preparations are interrupted briefly by the (mistaken) report that Don Pedro intends to propose marriage to Hero. What would be Leonato's reaction to having Don Pedro as his son-in-law? How does Leonato respond here? Why does he tell his brother to **Go you and tell her of it** *(line 17)* rather than doing it himself?

- Look carefully at Leonato's last speech in this scene (lines 15–20). Can you work out who his various remarks are addressed to and what each of them is about?

Don John

Most editions of *Much Ado About Nothing* identify Don John as **the Bastard** in the stage directions every time he appears on stage. However, it is not until Act 4 Scene 1 that his illegitimate birth is confirmed in the text when Benedick calls him **John the Bastard** *(line 183)* and characterises him as someone **Whose spirits toil in frame of villainies**.

He has been established as a malcontent (i.e. a discontented person) from the beginning of the play:

- Before the action starts he has led a rebellion against his brother, Don Pedro.

- Although **not of many words** he is now apparently **reconciled to the Prince your brother** *(Act 1 Scene 1, lines 114–16)*.

Act 1 Scene 3 reveals him as a stereotypical stage villain, jealous, dissatisfied, restless and vicious; he is an obsessive, dismissing pleas to **hear reason** *(line 5)* and dedicating himself to **build mischief** *(line 33)*.

Character

Begin to build up a **personality profile** on Don John:

- Notice how many times he uses the word 'I' between lines 8 and 28.

- Look at his choice of language, e.g. animals, food, images of restraint.

- Look at his views of Claudio, Hero, marriage, the **great supper** *(line 51)*.

Staging

In the opening scene Don John speaks only a few words.

If you were directing the play, how would you establish his character in the scene as a whole?

Write down your **working production notes**.

Consider such things as:

- costume – military (rebel uniform?), civilian, formal, casual?

- physical appearance – build, colouring, hair?

- voice – tone, delivery, accent?

- positioning on stage – involved, detached?

- manner – indifferent, watchful, sullen?

Whereas in the opening scene Don John had been only a marginal character, here he is the focal point of the scene.

- Does this scene require a change of mood from that of the first two scenes? Why?

- How would you manage a mood change: setting, lighting, sound effects, Don John's manner? What would Don John be doing?

Men's talk

Apart from Leonato, all of the main male characters in this first act have just returned from a military campaign. Depending on the style of the production they may well be dressed in military uniform, perhaps bearing the stains of battle and travel and carrying weapons.

The early speeches are about casualties and military prowess; Beatrice scornfully uses a fencing term – **Signor Montanto** – to refer to Benedick; the rivalry between Beatrice and Benedick is described in terms of **war** and **skirmish** *(lines 45–6)*; Claudio speaks of having previously viewed Hero with **a soldier's eye** *(line 219)*.

Cupid, the god of love, was used to advertise brothels.

This is very much a man's world and yet much of their conversation in this first act has been about women – particular women or women in general – and about marriage.

Their conversations often reveal contradictory attitudes but they all have a view of women that is essentially stereotypical: Angels or Whores.

It is significant that the subject of much of this debate – Hero – says not a word during the entire act!

Interpretation

1 Find evidence from Act 1 which suggests that men assume that women are:
   - shrewish
   - sexually immoral
   - admired for their beauty
   - prized for their chastity
   - valued for the money they will inherit
   - viewed as commodities
   - subject to having their feelings manipulated.

2 Make a note of one or more brief quotations to support each of the above points; record the speaker and act, scene and line number(s) of the quotation.

Most of the evidence will be in Act 1 Scene 1, but Scenes 2 and 3 also reinforce the attitudes established in the opening scene.

You will also find it helpful to read the Introductory Essay 1 'Women in a man's world' in the students' text.

Styles and titles

The world of *Much Ado About Nothing* is defined to a large extent by the social status of the characters:

- Don John is not referred to as 'the Prince' until Act 1 Scene 1, line 114 but the title 'Don' (meaning 'Sir') immediately identifies him as someone of high rank (interestingly the title has since been adopted as that of a high-ranking or powerful member of the Mafia in the United States) and he is routinely addressed as 'the Prince', 'my lord' or 'your grace'.
- When Leonato enquires about the casualties of war he is only interested in **How many gentlemen...** (i.e. men of rank) have been **lost**, and when he is told (mistakenly, as it turns out) that Don Pedro intends to propose marriage to his daughter, Hero, he warns her so that **she may be the better prepared for an answer'** (*Act 1 Scene 2, lines 16–17*). Marriage to the Prince would clearly bring enormous status to Leonato's family.
- Titles can be used mockingly – Benedick is **Signor Montanto** (*Act 1 Scene 1, line 23*), Beatrice is **my dear Lady Disdain** (*Act 1 Scene 1, line 88*) and later 'Count' Claudio is mocked as merely **Monsieur Love** (*Act 2 Scene 3, line 27*) – but even the kinship of the malcontent and illegitimate Don John is acknowledged as **my lord** (*Act 1 Scene 1, line 114; Act 1 Scene 3, line 1*) and later **Count John** (*Act 2 Scene 1, lines 9–10*).
- Often characters are referred to by 'titles' of kinship such as *cousin*, *niece* or *daughter*.

Language and Character

1 Make a list of the principal characters in the play in order of rank, beginning with Don Pedro, and allocate a separate sheet of paper to each character.

2 Draw up a table recording:
   a) the names or titles by which each is addressed
   b) the character using the name or title
   c) the act, scene and line reference
   d) the circumstances: formal, informal
   e) the tone in which the title is used: respect, affection, mockery, flattery
   f) the effect or implications of the usage where appropriate.

Example: Don Pedro

Name/Title	Character	Reference	Circumstances	Tone	Effect
'your grace'	Leonato	Act 1 Scene 1, line 73	Formal – host welcoming guest	Respect	Acknowledges Don John's rank and the demands of hospitality
'your grace'	Benedick	Act 1 Scene 1, line 152	Informal	Respect	Uses Don John's social and military rank as a lever to reveal Claudio's secret

Something and not[h]ing

In Shakespeare's time, 'nothing' was spoken much as we would pronounce the word 'noting' and is one of the **puns** which the title of the play exploits. While according to Beatrice, Benedick goes away with 'nothing' (line 48) at the conclusion of their battles of wits, Claudio begins by 'noting' Hero (line 119).

> A **<u>pun</u>** is a word or phrase which sounds the same as, or distorts the form of, another in a clever, witty or humorous way.

'Noting' has to do with 'observing', 'watching', 'spying' and involves 'reporting' what has been seen and heard – but watchers can be deceived and reports can be mistaken, mischievous or malicious.

The opening speeches of the play depend on matters reported by the Messenger – our first glimpse of Don Pedro, Claudio and Benedick is through the perspective of a third party. There is nothing sinister about the Messenger – but the reporting of second-hand information sets the tone for the rest of the play.

Any theatre audience is, of course, in a sense always 'spying' on the stage world and the characters that populate it.

Thus when Don Pedro suggests that he should impersonate Claudio and woo Hero on Claudio's behalf (see lines 241–49) we as audience are in a better position than any of the other characters in the play because we have actually been present. Happily, we know the truth!

The first of many examples of misunderstanding and misrepresentation occurs as early as Act 1 Scene 2 when Antonio tells his brother, Leonato, what one of his servants had told him about Don Pedro's intentions. This time the **strange news** *(line 3)* comes third-hand to Leonato!

☺ Interpretation and ☷ Structure

Draw up a diagram showing the misreporting episode in Act 1 Scene 2. Make sure you include:

a) the person(s) reporting

b) the person(s) receiving the news

c) the news itself

d) how it differs from the truth

e) whether the misreporting was a genuine mistake, mischievous or malicious

f) the effect(s) of the misreporting.

Set out your diagram in the way that you find most helpful: columns, spider plan, flow chart. Choose your diagram carefully – you will be using it again and will need to refer back to it – soon! 'Note' that Don John hopes his brother's 'wooing' of Hero **may prove food to my displeasure** (*Act 1 Scene 3, line 46*).

'Know me and not know me...' *(line 156)*

We have already touched on the Elizabethan pronunciation of the word 'nothing' in the play's title and 'noted' its connection with 'observing', 'watching' and 'spying' as well as with instances of reporting and – more commonly – mis-reporting.

You have also started to build up a database of related material in the form of a diagram based on the reporting to Leonato in Act 1 Scene 2 of Don Pedro's plan to woo Hero for Claudio (see Student Activities 7).

'The revellers are entering…'.

There are several other examples of this theme in Act 2 Scene 1 where the scope for misunderstanding and deception is obviously increased by the fact that identities are concealed behind masks. Some instances are trivial and playful; others significant and potentially dangerous. However, not all of the episodes here are examples of 'reporting'; often a character will have drawn a mistaken conclusion from his or her observations.

Structure

Using the same basic criteria that you used earlier (with minor amendments as necessary):

• plot in note form the following instances of misunderstanding or deception
• compare your notes with those of one or two other people
• transfer the new material to the diagram you created for Student Activities 7 and add new material as you come across it throughout the play. In this way you will build up a picture of the importance of the theme.

1 Leonato reminds us of his misunderstanding about the Prince's intentions (lines 48–9). How does he express this?

_____

_____

_____

2 The Prince's conversation with Hero (lines 61–71).
What does he believe?

_____

_____

What does she believe?

_____

_____

3 Ursula's conversation with Antonio (lines 82–91). Notice the twist in the pattern here: she knows who he is; he denies it.

_____

4 Beatrice's conversation with Benedick (lines 92–114).
What does she know?

_____

_____

_____

How does she use her knowledge?

_____

_____

_____

What does he believe?

_____

_____

_____

The Prince's jester.

How does this affect his behaviour (see also lines 155–60; 178–206)?

_____

_____

_____

5 Don John's conversation with Claudio (lines 115–39). This brings to a conclusion Don John's plot introduced in Act 1 Scene 3. There are variations on the bluff/counter-bluff theme here.

Who is genuinely deceived? _____

_____

How are the misunderstandings resolved as the scene unfolds?

_____

_____

_____

_____

6 As the malicious Don John plot is resolved, a more benign one begins to take its place. What is the plan? Who is involved? To be continued....

_____

_____

_____

_____

'...seeming truth...' *(line 33)*

Don John's first plan to cause trouble between his brother, Don Pedro, and Claudio over the wooing of Hero has mis-fired. In this scene he sets in motion a more malicious scheme with potentially tragic consequences.

Deception and misunderstanding are again the keys to Don John's plot; his victims will be misled by his lies and their own credulity.

Language

Towards the end of the scene Borachio sums up:

> **Be you constant in the accusation, and my cunning shall not shame me** *(lines 38–9)*

1 Look carefully at the ways in which language is distorted and values corrupted in this line: 'constancy' is a virtue but here it is corrupted by being applied to a false 'accusation'; 'cunning' is shameful but Borachio takes pride in upholding it.

This sums up the moral degeneracy of Don John and his accomplices; evil is applauded and virtue polluted. This immorality is expressed in images of disease.

2 See how many references to sickness and disease you can find.

_____

_____

3 Now note down occasions when ideas of 'honour', 'honesty', 'truth' and 'reputation' are used with reference to Claudio and Don Pedro in this scene. Why do you think this is?

_____

_____

4 Make a list of all of the words and phrases you can find in the scene that point up the central themes of deception and misunderstanding:

- **covertly** *(line 6)* • _____ • _____
- **misuse** *(line 20)* • _____ • _____

5 Make sure you understand the plot by making brief notes (with references where necessary) under the following headings:

- Who will do what? _____

   _____

- Who believes what? _____

   _____

- How are the practicalities to be managed? _____

   _____

Benedick and the 'love-gods'

Staging

You are going to think about staging one of Shakespeare's greatest comic scenes. This is one of the longest scenes in the play and is crucial to the comic plot: at the beginning of the scene Benedick is a confirmed bachelor; by its end he is **horribly in love** *(line 183)*.

Before looking at the actors' words and actions, however, give some time to the importance of setting the visual scene.

During the reign of Queen Elizabeth I, knot gardens became very popular in England. Most knot gardens were made with various herbs, or herbs and box. This woodcut is from the title page of Thomas Hill's 'The Gardener's Labyrinth' (1577).

Setting

Some productions place this scene in **the orchard** *(line 4)* though others have located it on a garden terrace or in 'another room' in Leonato's house.

The comedy of the scene depends largely on Benedick's being able to 'hide' from Don Pedro, Leonato and Claudio. It is also vital that the audience should be able to see his reactions to what is said about him.

Think about elements of set design that would help the actors to maximise the comedy: one production had Benedick hiding in a tree while smoking a cigar and peering through the leaves – and then choking on the smoke from his cigar and falling out of the tree.

Indoors: room design (alcoves, long curtains, stairs), items of furniture (settee, lounge chairs, bookcase, table).

Outdoors: garden benches, deckchairs, trellis screens, garden statuary, potted shrubs and trees, hedges.

Remember:

• A film production can use a different location for each new scene.

• On stage the play needs to flow smoothly from scene to scene without long delays for elaborate scene changes – the set would need to be substantially the same as that used for other scenes, perhaps with the addition of portable stage dressing.

• What sort of stage – proscenium (where the acting space is recessed behind an arch), thrust (where the acting space thrusts into the audience), arena (where the audience surrounds the stage)?

Discussion

Discuss these ideas and others of your own with the rest of the class and design a stage plan that you agree to accept as the basis for directing the actors.

It might be interesting to design both interior and outdoor settings with half of the class directing for each, and then comparing notes.

Costume

- How would you dress Benedick: dressing-gown, pyjamas, casual wear? Early in the scene Benedick ridicules Claudio who, like other young men in love, will **lie ten nights awake carving the fashion of a new doublet** (lines 13–14) – Benedick is obviously not very fashion-conscious.

The morning after…

- Would Benedick's costume contrast with that of the other male characters? Why might a contrast be effective? Would the military men now be in off-duty uniforms worn on 'leave' or in civilian dress (suits, tennis wear, riding gear, jeans and T-shirt, designer-casual)?

Discuss your ideas with one or two other people and then sketch and label costume designs for Benedick, Don Pedro, Claudio and Leonato (Leonato is older, of course) – or share the characters out between the group.

Performance

This is the first time we have seen the main characters since the evening of the masked party (Act 2 Scene 1).

- Is it 'the morning after the night before' – does Benedick have a hangover: dark glasses, glass of water and headache/indigestion tablets?
- Could there be other business going on around Benedick: servants clearing up after the party, vacuuming (how might Benedick react?), removing party decorations, arranging fresh flowers, laying the table, serving breakfast (Benedick's reaction)?
- What about the 'Boy'? Look at the Performance notes in your students' text and develop some comic business.

▦ Structure

The comedy depends partly on a series of comic contrasts between, for example:

- Benedick's exaggerated scorn of love and the speed with which he is converted into the conventional lover

- Benedick's belief that he is hidden from his friends and the fact that they know exactly where he is throughout the scene
- the 'ham' play-acting of Don Pedro and the others and Benedick's belief in their sincerity.

Discussion

Can you find other contrasts? What about Benedick's conversation with Beatrice in the scene's final episode, for example? What does each believe?

The audience's own position during the scene is a privileged one:

- We are in on the joke and enjoy being witnesses as the trick is played out.
- On a more sombre note, we also know of Don John's plan to destroy Hero's reputation and destroy Claudio's love (from Act 2 Scene 2).
  His method is exactly similar to that being used by his brother and the others to kindle the spark of love in Benedick.

Directing the scene

The scene falls broadly into five episodes:

- Benedick scorns Claudio's falling in love (lines 1–27)
- The musical episode – again Benedick mocks the conventional lover (lines 28–79)
- The gulling (tricking) of Benedick (lines 80–172)
- Benedick's immediate reaction (lines 173–90)
- Beatrice calls him to dinner (lines 191–203).

Choose one or two episodes from the scene (or divide up the whole scene into roughly equal sections.

Use a photocopy of your section of the scene and prepare a director's 'prompt copy' with notes and sketches. Characters can be identified by their initials and stage movement by arrows (colour-coded if necessary); notes on tone of voice, facial expression, gesture etc. can be written on the text side of the page with relevant text highlighted or underlined.

- Refer to your agreed stage plan.
- The 'Performance' features in your students' text should help with ideas.

For example: How does Benedick react when he first hears that Beatrice **should so dote on Signor Benedick** *(lines 84–5)*: astonishment, suspicion, smug satisfaction – all of these?

In one production Benedick spluttered and choked on a mouthful of wine; in another he flopped into a deckchair which collapsed under him.

Compare your ideas with those of others and try staging a short extract.

'...some with traps' *(line 106)*

Staging

a **gull**: someone who is easily fooled or cheated

The purpose of this scene – the **gulling** of Beatrice – closely parallels the previous one in which Benedick is tricked (Act 2 Scene 3) – it even takes place in the same setting. Many directors have made substantial cuts to the text to avoid labouring the joke.

- Using a photocopy of the scene, decide which lines and speeches you would cut while preserving both the comic plot and characterisation.
- How could you modify the look of the scene so as to give variety: different time of day (lighting?); incidental background business?
- Specific comic business: in one production Beatrice concealed herself behind a clothes-line full of washing; as she listened, Hero and Ursula piled sheet after sheet on her head so that she emerged for her soliloquy clutching a heap of linen. In another Beatrice emerged drenched after Hero had finished watering the vegetation behind which she was hiding.

Character

Both gulling episodes focus on the characters of the central (hidden) figures.

- Make a list of the characteristics catalogued by their respective friends under two headings. Keep a record of scene and line numbers.
- Which characteristics are referred to in both scenes?
- Which characteristics do Benedick and Beatrice apparently have in common?
- How do their characters differ, according to their friends?
- Are their friends' assessments of their characters accurate?

Where could you hide?

Benedick		Beatrice	
Characteristic	**Reference**	**Characteristic**	**Reference**
Scornful	2.3.146	Scornful	2.3.108; 3.1.61–68
Witty	2.3.151	Witty	3.1.52

Structure

There are obvious similarities between the two scenes. In both scenes:

- The central character hides.
- They each hear that they are loved by someone who had previously scorned them.
- They hear some unpleasant truths about themselves.
- There are disturbing echoes of the darker plot of Don John: Hero speaks of devising **some honest slanders / To stain my cousin with** *(lines 84–5)*; ironically she will herself soon be the victim of Don John's **dishonest slanders**. Can you find other **ironies**?

> **Irony**: the use of words to imply the opposite of what they normally mean

- They are initially sceptical but are soon convinced by what they have heard.
- Can you identify others?

What differences can you find between the two scenes?

Differences	Things to consider	Differences
1 **All-male characters**	• Do they all behave 'in character': Claudio, Leonato, Hero?	1 **All-female characters**
2 **Benedick provides a running commentary**	• To what effect?	2 **Beatrice is silent**
3 **Gulling stresses behaviour of Beatrice**	• Keep a record of reported behaviour and respective characteristics (with references)	3 **Gulling focuses on character**
4 **Scene begins in verse; gulling episode wholly in prose**	• Can you explain these differences? • How is rhyme is used in this scene? • Can you find other differences?	4 **Entire scene in verse** (Beatrice uses verse for first time)

Symptoms of love

🎭 Interpretation

When Benedick 'realised' that he had fallen in love with Beatrice he said that he expected to be the target of **some odd quirks and remnants of wit** (*Act 2 Scene 3, line 184*) because of his former scorn of love in general and Beatrice in particular.

List the various signs of love in Benedick that Don Pedro, Leonato and Claudio claim to have seen in Benedick (lines 1–52). Give a brief quotation (and line reference) to support each point.

Fashionable trends have often prompted ridicule. Here in 1869 men's flashy, tight trousers and fancy broad-shouldered jackets were mocked.

_____

_____

_____

_____

_____

💡 Staging

Why does Benedick say he has the toothache? Does it have anything to do with (a) his looking 'sadder' (b) his beard (c) another reason?

In one production, for example, Benedick had entered trying to sing 'Sigh no more, ladies' – a song he had scorned in Act 2 Scene 3 – in a cracked voice. When the others arrived he stuffed the words of the song into his mouth and tried to pass off the lump in his cheek as the toothache.

Look in detail at lines 11–22 (**Gallants, I am not ... he that has it**):

• How might his friends mock the 'new' Benedick – think about grouping and stage movement, tone of voice, facial expression, shared mock 'asides', comic by-play?

• How does Benedick react: does he 'play up' to the jokes; try to keep his dignity; is he embarrassed?

Divide out these lines and learn them if possible (no one has more than 3–4 lines) and experiment with different ways of presenting the episode.

If you have a performance space available, divide up the whole class into several groups and compare the performances.

Law and order

Context

There was no full-time police force at this time. Constables were local men elected (unpaid) for a year but it was a thankless public duty and many paid poor men like Dogberry and Verges to help them. They had no professional training, were often too old, lazy or incompetent to arrest thieves or stop fights and so were frequently a target for ridicule.

The Watch in *Much Ado About Nothing* could have been suggested by a similar group in John Lyly's play, *Endimion* (published in 1591) and many believe that Dogberry was based on a real constable.

Shakespeare's audiences would have known of the ineffectiveness of the Town Watch from their own experience and would have recognised and enjoyed seeing their failings ridiculed.

Hanging was the most common method of executing criminals and was regarded virtually as a spectator sport. More serious crimes involved slow death and mutilation.

1   Make a note of quotations about the uselessness of the Watch that would have had a topical appeal for Shakespeare's audience:

   • **We will rather sleep than talk; we know what belongs to a watch**
      (lines 28–9)

   • _____

   • _____

   • _____

2   The Constable explains to the Watch their duties. They are desperately anxious to 'get it right':

   a) Make a note of their queries.

   _____

   _____

   _____

   _____

   _____

   _____

   _____

b) How sensible are their answers?

_____

_____

_____

_____

_____

Much Ado About Nothing constantly gives us startling contrasts between comic and serious and this is true of the law-and-order theme too:

• The Watch are comic and often ridiculous – but they also capture the villains and bring them to justice.

• Notice, too, that although the play concludes with a double marriage and a 'happy ending', in the final line Benedick speaks of devising **brave punishments for Don John** *(Act 5 Scene 4, line 119)*. Don John will almost certainly be tortured and the play makes many other references to harsh punishments.

• Look up the following references and make a note of the punishments referred to:
  – Act 1 Scene 1, lines 171–2
  – Act 3 Scene 2, lines 16–19
  – Act 4 Scene 1, line 179
  – Act 5 Scene 1, lines 239–40.

You will also find it helpful to look at the Introductory essay 5 'Crime and punishment' in the students' text.

Mal à propos

🗨 Language

The word *malapropism* is not one that Shakespeare would have known. The word was coined after a character named Mrs Malaprop in a play called *The Rivals* (1775) by Thomas Sheridan. Her name comes from the French *mal à propos*, which means 'inappropriate'. The self-educated Mrs Malaprop was always substituting a similar-sounding word for the word that she intended to use.

Shakespeare used this technique for a number of characters. For example, the know-all character of Bottom in *A Midsummer Night's Dream* often uses the wrong word: **Thisby, the flowers of odious savors sweet** (*Act 3 Scene 1*).

Audiences in Shakespeare's day would have known that Bottom meant *odorous savors sweet* as in 'sweet smelling' and not *odious*, which means 'hateful' – not very romantic!

It is a device that is particularly effective when used by characters who have a high opinion of their own importance but are in fact ignorant and ill-educated. Shakespeare needed to appeal to the whole of his audience, both high- and low-born. Jokes based on classical literature and legend would have appealed to the educated members of his audience but Dogberry's 'howlers' would have appealed to all classes – and the spectacle of authority made ridiculous is a popular theme in every age.

In *Much Ado About Nothing* members of the Watch in general and Dogberry in particular are prone to this sort of verbal confusion. Dogberry is very conscious of the importance of his role as Constable so his ignorant slips make him appear even more ridiculous.

Refer to your students' text to make a list of some of his errors in this scene. Also give the word that was intended and explain why it is particularly inappropriate in its context:

- **senseless** (*line 16*) → sensible → Dogberry says that the constable of the Watch (who has authority over the others) is chosen *because* he's an idiot, i.e. he has been chosen because he is unsuitable!

- _____
  _____

- _____
  _____

- _____
  _____
  _____

Staging

The Watch scenes have traditionally been played with much slapstick business.

- Why should comedy be important at this point in the play? Look at what comes before and after this scene.

Sketch and label a costume for each member of the Watch.

Props corner. Some productions have portrayed the Watch in an incongruous mixture of costumes and with a bizarre assortment of weapons.

- How many members of the Watch are there? How are they identified? Could you give each his own character? What clues does the text offer?
  Dogberry's name suggests the fruit of the dogwood, round and red; Verges' name suggests 'verge', a staff of office, and therefore long and thin. What about the 'lesser' members of the Watch?

Divide out lines 1–73 and read the parts aloud two or three times, then devise some comic business.

- Are they reluctant or keen? Well-meaning but incompetent? Lazy and dim-witted? Sleepy? Drunk? A mixture of different attitudes?
- Dogberry is conscious of his own importance and believes himself to be very shrewd. Notice how the rivalry between Dogberry and Verges contributes to the humour. Verges' attempts to assert himself over Dogberry are a running joke in their scenes.
- How does Verges try to assert himself here and how does Dogberry react?

Discuss and then try one group reading the lines while another group acts the business.

The arrest

It is a wonderful irony that the least socially significant and apparently most incompetent characters in the play become the most important: whereas the 'elite' – Don Pedro and Claudio – are completely deceived by Don John, the members of the Watch recognise villainy when they hear it – and arrest the villains.

Messina TV News reports the capture of the villains and includes an interview with the officers and either CCTV footage with voiceover or a reconstruction of the arrest using extracts from Borachio's (and Conrade's?) speeches.

If you have a photocopy of the episode, go through and highlight the key information for the report as well as details of location, weather and behaviour. Below are some of the questions that will help you to structure your report. What else will you include?

- Write the script and a storyboard for this report.
- Try enacting the reconstruction over the report to be broadcast.

You could record the report onto audiotape.

(**'Here is the news…'**) (**Is Borachio drunk? Conrade? Both?**) (**What alerts the Watch?**) (**What do they do?**) (**What do they hear?**)

In or out?

⊞ *Structure*

This scene has often been cut in production. Why, do you think: is it too short; not much happens…?

Make out the best case you can for keeping it. Set out your ideas by expanding the director's notes below and adding ideas of your own:

Act 3 Scene 4: Before the wedding – IN or OUT?
Keep it in!

- *Scenes before and after?*
- *Effect of Margaret in scene? (NB Act 2 Scene 2, lines 9–35)*
- *Beatrice's cold – dramatic point! (NB its importance at Act 4 Scene 1, lines 142–4)*
- *Dramatic tension – we know what's coming!*
- *Contrast light and dark; joy and foreboding (NB lines 17 – and ???)*
- *Double love theme: Hero and Beatrice – different stages*
- *Develops Hero's character (NB her contribution – poignant: see Act 4 Scene 1)*
- *Pace – lively; excitement; anticipation (contrast ponderous Dogberry Act 3 Scene 5)*
-
-

🔦 *Staging*

Where would you stage this scene: Hero's bedroom, dressing-room? How would you dress the stage to suggest the location: dressing-table, wedding bouquet, various shoes, items of clothing, wedding cards?

Some productions have had business showing wedding preparations: one had a lady-in-waiting combing Hero's hair; another introduced comic business with Hero being laced into corsets. Can you suggest some comic business with Beatrice (she has a heavy cold)?

💬 *Language*

As final preparations for Hero's marriage are made, the talk turns to the age-old wedding subjects of clothes and sex – yet the mood of the scene shifts backwards and forwards between joy and apprehension.

The audience knows that Claudio intends to publicly condemn Hero during the wedding ceremony, so we recognise the significance of these fluctuating moods.

- Trace these shifts in atmosphere as the scene unfolds. *Hint:* look for words that reflect these two moods: light and dark; positive and negative. For example: **better** *(line 5)* – **not so good** *(line 7)*; **joy** *(line 17)* – **heavy** *(line 17)*:

'...great haste' – less speed

Staging

Divide into small groups of three or four as joint directors in early discussions about the staging of this scene. Prepare working notes to be passed on to each of the actors as well as to the costume and design teams. Consider the following:

1   The audience knows that the Watch's prisoners (Borachio and Conrade) have been overheard talking about the plot to shame Hero – and here is Hero's father talking to the very men who know this!

   • Could you have other preparations or activities going on off-stage (sound) or as background on-stage business to suggest this dramatic tension between the Watch's information and the imminent wedding?

   _____

   _____

   _____

2   Leonato is anxious to get ready for the wedding yet Dogberry and Verges repeatedly delay him.

   • How could you show this? Where is the scene set? What is Leonato doing – trying to tie a bow tie, learning/writing his speech?

   • Again Dogberry's and Verges' use of language obscures rather than explains – how?

   _____

   _____

   _____

3   Dogberry and Verges try to ingratiate themselves with the high-ranking Leonato.

   • In trying to impress Leonato how could they succeed only in irritating him? Unconsciously committing some social blunder?

   _____

   _____

   _____

4   There is rivalry between Dogberry and Verges as they compete with each other to tell their story – yet neither of them tells Leonato the details of what **decerns you nearly** (lines 2–3).

   • How could you show this rivalry: jockeying for position? facial expression? comic business? In one production they arrived on bicycles and Dogberry climbed through Verges' bicycle frame in his eagerness to deliver his news.

   _____

   _____

   _____

Plots in parallel

⊞ Structure

In Shakespeare's day plays were described in terms of their 'genre' or type: history, tragedy or comedy. However, Shakespeare's plays can rarely be pigeon-holed so easily into one category.

Much Ado About Nothing is primarily a comedy but the play also shows how fine is the dividing line between comedy and tragedy – in fact the two are often seen in parallel.

A series of eight posters issued in 1940 used cartoons to warn the public about the dangers of careless talk which could help the enemy. In this example the face of Adolf Hitler, the German leader, can be seen in the wallpaper design.

Much Ado About Nothing is like many of Shakespeare's plays in that there are two story lines – comic and tragic (or potentially tragic) – which may begin separately but which come together and overlap as the plot develops.

In order to weave these two very different strands into a unified whole Shakespeare often uses (a) themes (b) characters or (c) language in one plot which are matched – or contrasted – in the second plot.

Much Ado About Nothing has two main plots which both focus on the theme of love: the serious (potentially tragic) plot of Claudio and Hero, and the comic plot of Beatrice and Benedick.

Here are some examples of how Shakespeare builds matching or contrasting parallels into the two plots.

Themes: Deliberate deception – in the comic plot Don Pedro's light-hearted plan to deceive Beatrice and Benedick into love is matched in the serious plot by Don John's sinister scheme to slander Hero's honour. Don Pedro tries to bring Beatrice and Benedick together; Don John tries to drive Claudio and Hero apart.

Characters: Claudio quickly changes from soldier to lover – Beatrice and Benedick at first scorn love but quickly find themselves in love. Characters are vulnerable to deception or self-delusion – Benedick sees signs of love in Beatrice because he wants to, while Claudio believes what he sees at Hero's window because he fears to.

Language: Seeking confirmation of his choice, Claudio asks Benedick whether he had 'noted' (i.e. closely observed) Hero. Don John encourages Claudio to **trust that you see** *(Act 3 Scene 2, line 86)* in persuading him to doubt Hero; the Friar, however, is convinced of Hero's innocence by **noting of the lady** *(Act 4 Scene 1, line 153)*.

- Use the above examples as your starting point and make a note of other examples of parallel or contrasting elements as you study the play in more detail.

Dramatic irony

Dramatic irony has the effect of drawing us into the action of the play. It enables us to look forward eagerly to future events to see how they will work out.

> **Dramatic irony** occurs when the audience is given more information than one or more of the characters.

It is particularly effective in comedy – especially when a trick is being played on one or more of the characters. We enjoy the joke all the more if we are 'in the know': we watch as the bait is laid, see the victim caught in the trap and then enjoy seeing his or her reactions.

In *Much Ado About Nothing* some tricks are good-humoured and well-intended; others are vindictive and spiteful. Yet even the most light-hearted are tinged with a darker side: the comic plot to bring Beatrice and Benedick into **a mountain of affection, th'one with th'other** *(Act 2 Scene 1, line 271)* could be seen as a heartless deception – aren't their feelings, after all, being cruelly manipulated? At what point does a 'trick' become a 'plot'?

▦ *Structure*

So far three tricks or plots have been set up:

1 Don John's attempt to convince Claudio that Don Pedro had betrayed him in wooing Hero for himself.

2 Don John's plan to shame Hero and destroy Claudio's marriage.

3 Don Pedro's plan to bring about the marriage of Beatrice and Benedick.

- Sometimes the word 'trick' seems a better word to use than 'plot'. Why, do you think? Which of the following words would you apply to each of the three plots/tricks: *spiteful, mischievous, ingenious, callous, subtle, witty, humorous, wicked, unkind, clever, cruel*?

Look at each of the three plots in turn and ask yourself the following questions:

- Who is in on the plot/trick – and who isn't?

  1 _____

  2 _____

  3 _____

- Who is the main 'victim'? What reasons are given to justify the trick?

  1 _____

  2 _____

  3 _____

- Does the trick work? What steps do those playing the trick take to make sure that it works?

  1 _____

  2 _____

  3 _____

The happiest day…?

Performance

Almost the last words we heard Claudio speak had taken the form of a solemn pledge: **in the congregation where I should wed, there will I shame her** *(Act 3 Scene 2, lines 89–90).*

The audience knows what to expect in this scene and yet the dramatic impact of the rejection episode remains intense. How is the dramatic tension sustained?

1 Examine the first part of this scene, up to the departure of Claudio, Don Pedro and Don John (lines 1–107). With a partner, choose two or three of the following aspects of the episode and discuss the contribution that each makes to sustaining tension. Are there any other factors that contribute? Make notes (with references) on the following points and then share your thoughts with the rest of the class.

   • The build-up to the ceremony: music, procession, guests, flowers, costume.

   • The Friar's questions to the bride and groom.

   • The effect of Leonato's early responses (lines 1–66).

   • Language: contrast the use of the word 'maid' and language of purity with that of shame (e.g. **rotten orange**, *line 27*). Make a list and note who says what.

   • The way in which Claudio's denunciation of Hero is 'staged': has it been planned? Notice patterns of language, Don Pedro's and Don John's contributions, the movement from prose to verse. How does this affect your attitude to Hero and Claudio in particular?

2 At the beginning of the scene the audience knew what to expect. Once the shaming of Hero has taken place and Claudio and Don Pedro have left, the audience doesn't know what is going to happen. How is tension built up again during the second part of the scene?
   Again, choose from the following factors, discuss with a partner and then share your ideas with the class:

   • Hero's reaction – how are we kept guessing about her fate?

   • Leonato's response, particularly his language – is his reaction understandable, brutal, counter-productive, cruel, reasonable, selfish; what else?

   • The Friar's plan – What is he trying to do? Is his plan feasible, far-fetched, practical, fanciful, desperate, sensible? What do you think of his 'Plan B'?

   • Benedick's conversation with Beatrice.

Structure and Language

In the scene so far, cruel accusations have been made against Hero based on a mistaken or **false** 'observation' of Hero and Borachio.

The intervention of the Friar begins to restore a measure of reason and hope to the play. Appropriately his advice comes **By noting of the lady** *(line 153)* – in other words, from his true **observations** *(line 160)* of Hero.

3 Summarise in note form the Friar's plan (lines 195–249):

_____

_____

_____

_____

4 Insulting and destructive words were hurled at Hero in the early part of the scene. The Friar's 'observation' begins to redress the balance.

Make a record (with references) in this episode (lines 150–249) of positive examples of language used of both Hero herself and the hope of future harmony:

_____

_____

_____

_____

5 Don Pedro, Claudio and Benedick are close friends and comrades at the beginning of the play. Benedick is the first person to whom Claudio confides his love for Hero (see Act 1 Scene 1, lines 119–49) – but by the end of Act 5 Scene 1 Benedick will have challenged Claudio to a duel.

Note down the ways in which Shakespeare gradually distances Benedick from his friends. Ironically, good-natured fun sometimes contributes to the process. Look at the following:

• The trick to bring Benedick and Beatrice together.
• The comments about Benedick's character during the gulling scene (Act 2 Scene 3).
• Act 3 Scene 2: His friends' teasing of Benedick, the 'lover' – is Benedick himself changing?
• Claudio and Don Pedro do not confide to Benedick their belief in Hero's unfaithfulness – why, do you think?
• Act 4 Scene 1: Benedick stays when Claudio and Don Pedro leave the 'wedding' after shaming Hero – a moment of decision for Benedick?
• Benedick's responses to Hero's despair – a more serious, responsible Benedick?

A woman's role

Character and **Context**

For many women marriage was their expected objective in life; it was being a wife that gave her life meaning and reason. (See the Introductory Essays 1 'Women in a man's world' and 2 'Wooing and wiving' in the students' text.)

The ducking stool was just one of the humiliating punishments reserved for a 'shrew' or 'scold'.

- When Leonato tells Beatrice **thou wilt never get thee a husband if thou be so shrewd with thy tongue** (*Act 2 Scene 1, lines 14–15*) he warns that unless she changes her ways she will have failed in her life's main purpose.

- The criticisms made of Beatrice's character by Hero and Ursula in the gulling scene (Act 3 Scene 1) can be seen as warnings to women in general against displaying such qualities as 'pride' and 'scorn'.

However, for much of the play Beatrice has not behaved 'in role' – that is, as a woman was expected to behave.
- She has poured scorn on men in general and on the idea of marriage.
- She has exchanged bawdy witticisms with men.
- She has upheld strong personal opinions.
- She has defended her position vigorously when urged to be more conventionally 'feminine'.

1   Find examples (with references) of these aspects of Beatrice's character and behaviour.

_____

_____

_____

_____

2   Are there any other ways in which she behaves out of role?

_____

_____

_____

3   Make a note of ways in which Hero is contrasted with Beatrice in fulfilling the conventional woman's role:

_____

_____

_____

_____

Character and **Language**

Nevertheless, as soon as Beatrice *overhears* herself described in these terms she immediately 'falls into line' with the conventional female role:

> **Stand I condemned for pride and scorn so much?**
> **Contempt, farewell! And maiden pride, adieu!**
> **No glory lives behind the back of such** *(Act 3 Scene 1, lines 108–10)*

For the first time she becomes aware of what people say about her 'behind the back' – in other words, her reputation.

- Is this the same sort of 'reputation' that Don John's plot has sought to destroy in Hero?
- What are the main differences between 'male' and 'female' notions of honour?
- Is Beatrice's use of **glory** *(line 110)* a 'masculine' word? Is it closer to the masculine notion of 'honour' and 'good name' than the feminine?

At the end of Act 4 Scene 1 (lines 250–312) Beatrice and Benedick are left alone for the first time as 'lovers'. It is very different from a conventionally 'romantic' meeting. The audience wants to see them 'get together' – but the minds and feelings of Beatrice and Benedick are in a whirl as they struggle to reconcile their new feelings for each other with the traumatic events that have just taken place.

Show how Shakespeare uses the tension in this episode between love and hate, friendship and animosity, to show two people being pulled in opposite directions by their feelings. Look at the following:

- Where in the episode does Benedick try to bring the conversation round to the subject of love? What is Beatrice's response?

_____

_____

- Three times Beatrice says **O (God) that I were a man!** – why?

_____

_____

- Note down any language used by Beatrice that seems essentially masculine, even brutal. How do you explain this?

_____

_____

- Make a note of how references to lovers' promises and the swearing of oaths are used. How are they connected to 'honour' and 'reputation'?

_____

_____

- What is the impact of Beatrice's line **Kill Claudio** *(line 277)?*

_____

_____

- Do you think that Beatrice manipulates Benedick's feelings? How?

_____

_____

          Nelson Thornes Shakespeare: *Much Ado About Nothing* © Lawrence Green, Nelson Thornes Ltd, 2004

The examination

▐▐▐ Structure **Performance**

In this scene Shakespeare combines comedy and intense drama. Will the truth emerge before Benedick and Claudio fight in a deadly duel?

Off-stage: the events of the previous scene have brought disgrace, alienation, a reported death, the pledge of a duel, a declaration of love and a glimmer of hope.
On-stage: the truth gradually begins to emerge – but with nail-biting slowness.

The drama

Remind yourself of the dramatic events from Act 4 Scene 1 which provide background tension to this scene, by making notes (with brief quotations) under each of these headings:

- Disgrace
- Alienation

- Reported death
- Pledge of duel

- Declaration of love
- Glimmer of hope.

The comedy

Shakespeare builds tension by slowing the pace of the scene and delaying the exposure of the truth about Don John's plot. Find examples of how this is done through:

- Dogberry's misuse of language
- his failure to discriminate between important and trivial matters
- his ignorance of legal procedure.

Where and how does the pace of the scene quicken?

_____

_____

_____

◖ Character and **◖ Staging**

Once the truth is out and the Sexton exits to seek out Leonato there is a tremendous sense of relief and the scene ends with pure comedy created by Dogberry at his own expense.

Dogberry is a ridiculous figure – but does he also deserve our sympathy?

Discussion

Discuss the last section of the scene (lines 53–68) with a partner:

- What makes him ridiculous?
- What makes him deserve sympathy?

How would you stage the last twenty lines of the scene to bring out the pathos as well as the comedy of Dogberry's position?

Age before duty?

Language

- In the main quarrel between Leonato/Antonio and Claudio/Don Pedro, each
  side is convinced of the rightness and justice of its own position.
  Find a brief quotation (and line reference) which illustrates the rightness of
  each side's position:

  _____

  _____

  _____

- The quarrel between them focuses largely on the issue of 'age versus youth'.
  Note down the references to youth or age:

  _____

  _____

  _____

- Both sides draw on stereotypical ideas about the behaviour and attitudes of the
  different generations. Find examples and write an explanation by looking at
  your gloss notes if the modern meaning is not obvious:

Youth	*Age*
Fashion-mongering boys *(line 94)*	**I speak not ... under privilege of age to brag**
	What I have done being young *(lines 59–61)*

  _____

  _____

Staging

- Some productions have made the old men
  ridiculous, others almost tragic figures: one
  Leonato could not get his sword out of its
  scabbard; another chased Claudio around
  the stage and threw an umbrella at him.

- Some productions have made the young
  men callously taunting or contemptuous,
  others cold and unfeeling.

How could these interpretations be suggested by
stage business and the way the lines are delivered?

IF ONLY THESE KIDS HAD GROWN UP WITH
THE SAME ROLE MODELS WE HAD, THEN
MAYBE THEY WOULDN'T LOOK SO DAMN
RIDICULOUS!

DADDY   MUMMY

MOORE

*The inevitable gulf between old
and young.*

Choose a short extract from the episode and divide out the parts. Discuss and
rehearse comic and serious versions of the same lines.

📖 Context

In Shakespeare's play *As You Like It* the character Jacques reflects upon a man's life and compares it to an actor playing a variety of parts on the stage of life:

An illustration of The Seven Ages of Man from a book by the thirteenth-century scholar Bartolomaeus Anglicus (Bartholomew the Englishman), published in 1482.

The Seven Ages of Man

All the world's a stage,
And all the men and women merely players,
They have their exits and entrances,
And one man in his time plays many parts,
His acts being seven ages. At first the infant,
Mewling and puking in the nurse's arms.
Then, the whining schoolboy with his satchel
And shining morning face, creeping like snail
Unwillingly to school. And then the lover,
Sighing like furnace, with a woeful ballad
Made to his mistress' eyebrow. Then a soldier,
Full of strange oaths, and bearded like the pard,
Jealous in honour, sudden, and quick in quarrel,
Seeking the bubble reputation
Even in the cannon's mouth. And then, the justice
In fair round belly, with good capon lin'd,
With eyes severe, and beard of formal cut,
Full of wise saws, and modern instances,
And so he plays his part. The sixth age shifts
Into the lean and slipper'd pantaloon,
With spectacles on nose, and pouch on side,
His youthful hose well sav'd, a world too wide,
For his shrunk shank, and his big manly voice,
Turning again towards childish treble, pipes
And whistles in his sound. Last scene of all,
That ends this strange eventful history,
Is second childishness and mere oblivion,
Sans teeth, sans eyes, sans taste, sans everything.
(As You Like It, Act 2 Scene 7)

- Make a list of the seven ages and list the characteristics of each age.
- Which of Shakespeare's 'ages' still apply today – and which have changed?
- Into which age would you place Benedick, Don John, Antonio, Leonato, Claudio? Do any of these characters seem to occupy more than one 'age' during the play?
- In Shakespeare's day a woman would have had no career or profession and would probably have had only four 'ages' – infant, child, wife, widow. What 'ages' could a modern woman have?

'Too wise to woo peaceably...' *(line 52)*

Language

At the opening of the scene (lines 1–15) Benedick and Margaret engage in a form of **merry war** that Benedick had previously enjoyed with Beatrice. The language is mainly military with strong sexual **innuendo**. Use the gloss notes in the students' text to identify and explain the way they use language here.

> **Innuendo**: an indirect or subtle reference

Word/Phrase	Explanation
come over *(line 6)*	(i) Write better verse in praise of Margaret's beauty. (ii) Mount her sexually.

During this exchange with Margaret:

- Does Benedick enter into the banter as enthusiastically as previously – or is he slow to respond to Margaret's wit? Find evidence.

- Who do you think gets the better of this verbal duel? What is the evidence?

However, when Margaret leaves to fetch Beatrice, Benedick reflects (lines 16–29) on his lack of success in using the conventional 'language' of the courtly lover in singing and writing love poetry.

- What do you think is wrong with his efforts? How does he explain his lack of success?

Different species?

The time that Benedick and Beatrice spend together in this scene (lines 30–77) is only the second – and final – time that they are alone as 'lovers' in the play.

Character

Remind yourself of the previous occasion they were alone together (see Act 4 Scene 1, lines 250–312).

- Make a note of the circumstances on that occasion that made it difficult for them to focus on their developing relationship. Support your comments with brief quotations:

_____

_____

_____

For most of this meeting Beatrice and Benedick do not realise that the truth about Don John's plot has been revealed (see Act 5 Scene 1) and serious matters again hinder their love-making.

- Note down with brief quotations (a) the issues and (b) the language which convey a sense of underlying seriousness to the meeting:

  a) **Issues**

_____

_____

_____

  b) **Language**

      e.g. **foul words** *(lines 36 and 37)*; **suffer love** *(lines 46 and 47)*

_____

_____

_____

Again the two lovers are sparring – **Thou and I are too wise to woo peaceably** *(line 52)* says Benedick – but they are not now at 'war'. The earlier sexual aggression has begun to develop into something more mature.

- Compare the way they talk to each other now, in Act 5 Scene 2, with earlier in the play in Act 1 Scene 1 and Act 2 Scene 1.
- How does the tone of Benedick's encounter with Margaret at the beginning of Act 5 Scene 2 differ from his conversation with Beatrice later in the same scene?
- Where does Beatrice and Benedick's conversation seem awkward, embarrassed, coy, relaxed, affectionate, flirtatious, subdued, passionate? Explain the different tones.
- How has their relationship changed since their last meeting?
- How is their wooing different from the conventional courtly lover that Benedick had (unsuccessfully) tried to imitate earlier with his love poems and self-conscious attention to his appearance?

Dear Director...

Staging

This short scene has often been cut in stage productions. What do you think is its value?

Imagine that you are a theatre critic who has just been to Press Night of a production of the play by a leading professional company. You were disappointed to find that the scene was omitted by the director.

- Write a letter to the director expressing your disappointment and urging him or her to restore it before the production goes on tour. Expand on the following notes that you jotted down at the time. Can you think of any other points?

Dear ......

I was a member of the audience at last night's Press Night

performance of 'Much Ado' and was disappointed to find......

Notes: 5.3 – What happened to it...?

- *Impressive staging – spectacle (see Production suggestions in text).*

- *Imp. transition: broken wedding ➜ festivities in 5.4*

- *Chance 4 Claudio 2 redeem 'self' – otherwise not worthy of Hero? NB Last time we saw Cl. + Don J. = 5.1 – not flattering.*

- *Solemnity contrasts end 5.2 & start 5.4*

- *Sugg. hope + new beginning – N.B. D. Pedro's lines 24–31.*

- *Varies pace – slows before final sprint to the finish*

And all lived happily...?

⊞ Structure Performance

Shakespeare rarely does the obvious; he often leaves tantalising question marks that leave us wondering about the future...

Will Benedick's friendship with Claudio and Don Pedro ever be the same? Are they fully reconciled in this final scene?

Happy Ending...?

The final scene of the play resolves the various misunderstandings that have driven the plot forward and it ends with the prospect of a double marriage and a conventional 'happy ever after' ending...

...OR DOES IT...?

- Look carefully at lines 40–51: are their exchanges entirely good-humoured? Is there still some resentment between them? Benedick seems to want to put all bitterness behind them: **Come, come we are friends** *(line 111)*? Will Claudio accept the gesture? He doesn't say anything!

Beatrice and Benedick now finally realise that they were tricked into love – or do they?

- Look again at Benedick's dialogue with Leonato (lines 21–32), particularly line 27; and the lovers' exchanges at lines 71–84 – note the repetition of **they swore...** . How will Beatrice and Benedick react when they are finally alone together?

Beatrice is unusually quiet after line 95: Benedick's line **I will stop your mouth** effectively silences her for the rest of the play.

- Is she still puzzling about the trick played on herself and Benedick? Do you think she will now become the conventional silent and obedient wife that seems to have been the Elizabethan ideal?

What about Don Pedro? His seems to be the only **sad** *(line 115)* face at the end of the play, while the joyous final moments are marred briefly by the news of his brother's capture and Benedick's threat of **brave punishments for him** *(lines 119–120)*.

- Benedick encourages Don Pedro to **get thee a wife**. Will Don Pedro marry, do you think?

The play began against the background of a military campaign against the forces of the illegitimate malcontent Don John and the hope that he was now **reconciled** with his brother *(Act 1 Scene 1, line 114)*. Do you think he will ever be reconciled? Does Don Pedro foresee future conflicts with Don John?

1   Allocate parts to members of your class and arrange a **tableau** (performers 'frozen' in position) as if for a wedding photograph. Use grouping, body language and facial expression to suggest some of the issues outlined above. You could use two separate groups and each try to guess the other's characters.

   If possible take an actual photograph to see how successful you have been.

2   Write a plot outline for the sequel to the play, *Much Ado About Nothing – Part 2*.

   Use the characters that Shakespeare has created in *Part 1* and some of the ideas on this page for developing the story line.

Give us the money!

Language

Theatres, like professional football clubs, try to subsidise their activities by marketing and selling merchandise. The National Theatre, Shakespeare's Globe and The Royal Shakespeare Company, for example, all sell products to visitors and tourists ranging from programmes and posters to tea towels and key rings.

Find brief quotations from the play that would be suitable and amusing to print on the following items in a theatre shop. For example, **If he be sad, he wants money** (*Act 3 Scene 2, line 15*) might be suitable for a wallet or chequebook case.

- A sweatshirt
- A diary
- A pen set
- Boxer shorts
- A computer mouse mat
- A pack of notelets
- A key ring
- A sports bag
- Deodorant
- Socks
- A fridge magnet.

Can you add other items to the theatre's shop catalogue?

Design an A3 poster and/or an A4 programme cover for a production of *Much Ado About Nothing*. Incorporate into your design a number of brief quotations from the play and include visual elements that suggest one or more of the play's themes. You might try a collage-effect combining your own graphics with elements taken from magazines.

Design your own version of the cover for the students' text of the play with an appropriate quotation.

Design and write the viewing notes for a DVD version of the play to include the following:

- Chaptering using your own chapter titles.
- A lively summary of the plot using not more than 200 words.
- A cast list of the characters in the play chosen from among your favourite film and TV actors, entertainers and sports personalities. 'Write up' some of the key performances on the DVD in suitably glowing terms.

Are you an ageist?

Context

Some of the issues in *Much Ado About Nothing* are presented in terms of differences between the generations. Remind yourself of the confrontation between old and young in Act 5 Scene 1.

Newspaper and magazine articles often use headlines that draw attention to the age of the people in the articles:

Have-a-go Granny foils thief

Alarming rise in Teen STDs

Pensioners wed in haste

Gymslip Mums at Risk

Fittest Fifties Fight the Flab

Youths Heroes in Bus Tragedy

As a class make two different poster-sized collages entitled 'Youth' and 'Age'. Use a mixture of sketches, graphics and pictures and lettering cut from newspapers and magazines.

You might use the following questions as the basis for choosing material for your posters or for a class discussion on the subject.

- Who do you regard as the 'older generation': older brothers/sisters, teachers, parents, grandparents? What makes someone 'old' – is it just their actual age? Does it have to do with their attitudes?

- Do you ever feel that the older generation make certain assumptions about you and young people in general? Such as? Are their assumptions ever justified – be honest!

- Do you think you have stereotypical views of old people? When does someone become 'old' for example? How do you expect 'old' people to behave, dress, move, speak? Do the 'old' people that you actually know really conform to your notion?

Which aspects of being 'young' will you be glad to leave behind? Are there any advantages of being 'old'?

Ageless stories

⊞ Structure

Shakespeare very rarely invented his own plots. Usually he found stories that had been around for many years and were well known to his Elizabethan audiences. He often blended bits of several stories and wove them into something rich and new that his own audiences could relate to – in other words he updated them.

The plot of *Much Ado About Nothing* has several elements that had been around for a long time, sometimes for centuries:

- The slander of a chaste woman. The biblical story of Susannah and the Elders in the **Apocrypha** would have been one of the best-known examples.

> **Apocrypha**: books included as an appendix to the Old Testament

- A lover is deceived into believing that his beloved is unfaithful. This story goes back at least to late classical times. Shakespeare seems to have drawn particularly on two Italian versions of the story published in the sixteenth century for the Hero–Claudio plot.

- The role of Beatrice and Benedick, wittily scorning the idea of love and romance, was also well established in the sixteenth century. However, an important stimulus for Shakespeare may have been one of the most widely-read books of the century, the Italian Baldassare Castiglioni's *The Book of the Courtier* (1528). This incorporated the revolutionary idea that women had much to contribute to courtly life and included a series of lively debates on the subject between a man and woman.

- Humorous constables characterised by confused speech and ludicrous logic were long-established theatrical characters, though Dogberry was probably created especially for the principal comic actor in Shakespeare's company, Will Kempe.

Choose one of the plot lines in *Much Ado About Nothing* and write your own story and do what Shakespeare did, bringing it up to date for modern times.

You might try one of these ideas – or find another theme from the plot:

- Friends divided by jealousy, suspicion or misunderstanding.
- Someone mistakenly believes their girlfriend or boyfriend is two-timing them.
- Friends decide to bring together a boy and girl who normally don't get on.
- Pushy parents: Hero meekly accepts her father's ideas about 'marrying well'. A modern daughter might not be so co-operative.

Shakespeare uses the eavesdropping method to develop his story lines, and in other plays letters are used to trick lovers, but you could introduce modern technology for seeing and listening: CCTV, mobile phones, texting, picture messaging, camcorders, chat rooms…

Here comes the bride

Context

A wedding is always an important personal and, usually, family event. In Shakespeare's day marriage – particularly between wealthy, influential families – often had more to do with safeguarding property and investments than with love yet the virginity of the bride was paramount. Without it she was 'worthless'. Look again at the Introductory Essay 2 'Wooing and wiving' in the students' text.

In modern times the marriage of a famous personality from the world of sport or entertainment can acquire the quality of pure theatre, with the media 'performance' exceeding the significance of the ceremony itself.

A dramatic wedding scene has also been an indispensable element in the plots of countless novels, films and TV soaps.

The press often revel in 'naming and shaming' public figures whom they see as having broken some important moral code.

1   Can you think of examples of these?

_____

_____

_____

2   Devise and write an article to accompany a personality wedding of your choice (or invention) for a lifestyle or celebrity gossip magazine. Find suitable pictures and adopt an appropriate 'house style'.

3   Design and write the front page of the tabloid *Messina Star* or broadsheet *Messina Times* the day after Hero's 'wedding', using appropriate headlines.

4   It is common for a wedding to be photographed and videoed during the ceremony. Imagine that the official photographer had continued to take pictures during the dramatic events of this scene.

  - Divide the class into two – or more – groups and allocate the named characters and unnamed relatives and other guests to the members of each group.

  - Choose dramatic moments in the scene (up to the point where Hero faints) and arrange or stage them as powerful photographic 'stills'. You might be able to take your own digital photos.

  - Compare the results of the two groups and try to work out who is who in each 'picture'.

Baiting Benedick

Copy down a number of Benedick's anti-marriage/anti-Beatrice quotations from the early part of the play that his friends could use to remind him of his former attitude.

1 Which would be suitable for the following?

- A slogan worn on a T-shirt
- A note left on his pillow
- A post-it note attached to his computer

2 Use some of the quotations as the basis for a send-up of Benedick in one of the following:

- a rap song
- a love song with guitar accompaniment modelled on Balthasar's song in Act 2 Scene 3
- a mobile text message (in text spelling and maximum 160 characters).

3 Design a spoof Valentine's Day card from Benedick to Beatrice with suitable graphics and 'romantic' verse.

4 Design a mock-up of a leaflet or flyer announcing the engagement of Benedick and Beatrice and inviting all-comers to the wedding.

5 Prepare an audio or video 'dating profile', supposedly about Benedick, detailing his qualities as an eligible husband.

6 Later in the play (Act 5 Scene 2, lines 16–29) Benedick admits that he has tried to write a love poem to Beatrice but comes to the conclusion that he was **not born under a rhyming planet**. Using the clues he gives, write your own version of his poem.

7 You have been asked to be Benedick's 'best man'. Write the opening paragraphs of your speech at the wedding reception, giving suitable attention to the groom's confirmed bachelor days.

After the show...

Structure

It is sometimes interesting to imagine that the characters we have got to know so well during the play have independent lives that continue after the various threads of the plot have been drawn together at the end of the performance.

Here are a number of possible scenarios that you might like to explore further. You can probably think of others of your own.

- Dogberry meets up in the pub with the other members of the Watch after Borachio and Conrade have been handed over to Leonato.

- Ursula presses Margaret for the gossip about her relationship with Borachio and the 'incident' in Hero's bedroom.

- Don Pedro visits his bastard brother, Don John, in prison.

- Leonato and his brother, Antonio, relax once the double wedding is over and all the guests have gone.

- The musician, Balthasar, has performed on two important occasions: setting the scene for the trick played on Benedick (Act 2 Scene 3); and singing a solemn tribute to Hero (Act 5 Scene 3). What does he have to say about these things when next drinking with the musicians who had played at the masked party?

- Meanwhile, back at the monastery, Friar Francis enjoys telling his story to the other monks.

- Borachio and Conrade, in adjoining cells, ponder their position and apportion blame.

- At the end of the play Benedick urges Don Pedro to **get thee a wife**. The Prince thinks about it!

- After their wedding Beatrice and Benedick finally get round to discussing the circumstances that brought them together as lovers.

Try writing down a draft of how the conversation might develop and then improvise the scene. If time allows you could script it more fully.

Hearing the play

Language

Whereas today we probably speak of going to 'see' a play, Shakespeare's audiences would have spoken of going to 'hear' a play. With little in the way of scenery or stage effects they depended very much on the words to create the images that a modern production will create with scenery, lighting and sound. They would therefore have been more attuned than a modern audience to the different rhythms and cadences of the dialogue.

Much Ado About Nothing is relatively unusual among Shakespeare's plays in that much of the dialogue – some two-thirds – is spoken in prose. This is because the play is primarily a comedy and much of the dialogue is essentially social, light-hearted and informal.

Prose was the traditional vehicle for comedy and was typically spoken by low-status characters such as Dogberry and the members of the Watch but in this play even the high-status characters speak prose when they are relaxed. Their prose, however, is of a particularly structured and elegant form with elements usually found in verse: imagery, balanced phrases, rhythms, repetitions and **antitheses** (pairs of contrasting or opposite words used for effect).

It is common in Shakespeare's plays for 'noble' characters – whether noble by virtue of their birth or their moral qualities – to be 'dignified' with the addition of verse. In *Much Ado About Nothing*, however, even the high-class characters like the Prince, Count Claudio and Leonato, Governor of Messina, are given verse only on 'special' occasions.

In Act 1 Scene 1, for example, when Claudio, Benedick and Don Pedro are joking about love and marriage they use prose; as soon as Benedick has left and Claudio asks Don Pedro for serious advice on the same subject they instantly adopt verse.

Verse tends to be reserved for occasions that are serious, formal or have moral 'weight' – though even the wicked Don John can speak verse when he is pretending to adopt the moral high ground (see his contributions to the denunciation of Hero in Act 4 Scene 1).

When Shakespeare employs verse he normally writes in **iambic pentameter** or **blank verse**. This refers to a basic line-length of ten syllables with five strong beats and *without* rhyme: if it rhymes it's not blank verse!

However, there are often variations on the basic 'five-beat', ten-syllable pattern. English is a rich and highly flexible language and an unvaried regular line pattern would sound artificial and stilted. The 'five-beat' metre, however, remains as a basic background rhythm.

> **Iambic pentameter** is a verse line consisting of five iambs, or metrical units. Each unit (or 'foot') has an unstressed syllable followed by a stressed syllable, producing a 'de-dum' pattern of sound. **Pent-** is from the Greek word *penta* meaning five.

Read the following lines from Act 1 Scene 1, the first lines of blank verse in the play. Notice which lines fit the iambic 'de-**dum**' pattern most neatly – and which do not. The first four lines are shown here with the stressed syllables in bold type:

CLAUDIO	My **liege**, your **high**-ness **now** may **do** me **good**.
DON PEDRO	My **love** is **thine** to **teach**; teach **it** but **how**,
	And **thou** shalt **see** how **apt** it **is** to **learn**
	An-y **hard less**on that may **do** thee **good**.
CLAUDIO	Hath Leonato any son, my lord? 215
DON PEDRO	No child but Hero, she's his only heir.
	Dost thou affect her, Claudio?
CLAUDIO	O my lord,
	When you went onward on this ended action,
	I looked upon her with a soldier's eye,
	That liked, but had a rougher task in hand 220
	Than to drive liking to the name of love…

- Notice that 'Claudio' is spoken as two syllables, not three: **Claud**-io rather than **Claud**-i-o.

- Notice also that in line 217 the first part of the line (seven syllables) is spoken by Don Pedro and the final three syllables are spoken by Claudio.

- Line 218 has eleven syllables which suggests the urgency of Claudio's love.

- Claudio's picking up and completing Don Pedro's line and the extra syllable also conveys a sense of the young man's eagerness.

- When Shakespeare alters the regular iambic pentameter line it is usually because he wants to give certain words a particular emphasis or urgency.

All change…!

Shakespeare switches between prose and verse as part of the dramatic construction of entire scenes. The gulling of Benedick (Act 2 Scene 3) is mainly in prose that encourages a more humorous and boisterous playing of the scene. The gulling of Beatrice, however, is entirely in verse and is played more 'feelingly' and with less comic business.

- Notice that in the scene in which Benedick is tricked (Act 2 Scene 3) Don Pedro, Claudio and Leonato begin in verse – they are preparing the ground for the gulling of Benedick with romantic verse-talk.

- Look carefully at Act 4 Scene 1 in which Hero is denounced. The early stages of the ceremony are in prose which suggests normality; the solemn public denunciation of Hero and its life-changing repercussions require the serious medium of verse. The contrast is all the more effective.

- Beatrice and Benedick instinctively speak in prose which suits their sceptical worldly-wise outlook on life and love. However, even they sometimes use verse at dramatically intense moments.

Gods and heroes

Language and **Context**

In Shakespeare's day the ruling classes were beginning to see the value of education and were encouraged in the study of Latin, rhetoric and the classical authors where they learned about the gods and myths of Ancient Greece and Rome.

Much Ado About Nothing abounds in exchanges between cultured, educated men and – in the case of Beatrice – women who play elaborate, witty verbal games, drawing on their classical knowledge to score points and so light-heartedly maintain status within their social circle. Here are some of the most important examples.

The gods

- **Cupid** (see Act 1 Scene 1, lines 183–5) and **Venus** (see Act 4 Scene 1, lines 55–6)

  The classical god mentioned most in the play is, of course, Cupid. This is to be expected in a story in which love plays such an important part.

  Cupid was the Roman god of love and the son of Venus, the goddess of love, and these two figures were hugely popular in the poetry, literature and art of Shakespeare's time.

  The Ancient Romans often showed Cupid as a winged child or baby who carried a bow and quiver full of arrows. Cupid was also often represented as being blind, so it is hardly surprising that his love arrows hit people who were not suited to each other.

- **Diana** (see Act 4 Scene 1, lines 52–3; Act 5 Scene 3, lines 12–21)

  Diana had many identities but she was mainly seen as the moon goddess, goddess of chastity – and therefore in direct opposition to Venus, goddess of love. She was also associated with hunting and (strangely) marriage and childbirth.

  In *Much Ado About Nothing* references to Hero – whether ironic or literal – as a model of purity and virginity naturally see her as serving Diana, the patroness of virgins.

The rape of Europa.

- **Zeus** (i.e. **Jove**) and **Europa** (see Act 5 Scene 4, lines 43–51)

  Jove delighted in coming down to earth in a variety of disguises, usually in the pursuit of lovers.

  In Greek mythology Europa was a beautiful Phoenician princess. Zeus (or Jove) saw her gathering wild flowers and immediately fell in love with her. Zeus transformed himself into a white bull and carried Europa away to the island of Crete where he revealed his true identity. Europa became the first queen of Crete and had several children by Zeus.

Heroes and heroines

- **Hero and Leander** (see Act 4 Scene 1, line 95)

  Leander fell deeply in love with the beautiful Hero but she was a priestess to the goddess Aphrodite. Marriage was therefore impossible but they agreed to meet secretly. Every night Hero placed a lamp in the top of the tower where she dwelt by the sea, and Leander, guided by it, swam across the dangerous Hellespont – the stretch of water marking the boundary between Asia and Europe – to be with her. One stormy night the lamp was blown out and Leander drowned. On finding his body next morning on the shore, Hero flung herself into the waves.

  The story was widely used as a model of faithful love. In *Much Ado About Nothing* the legend would have given extra significance to the character called Hero, and the doubts about her faithfulness.

Planets and personality

Context

On one level *Much Ado About Nothing* is concerned with the disruption and restoration of order and harmony. Disorder in the state through Don John's rebellion provides the background for widespread disorder and confusion in the personal lives of the characters. Eventually, however, a measure of harmony is restored.

The idea of harmony or order was central to the mind-set of an Elizabethan. The universe was seen as interconnected at every level with human beings for whom, according to the Book of Genesis in the Bible, the universe had been created. Actions in the heavens produced reactions on the earth and these reactions might be felt both in the body politic (i.e. the state) and in the body of the individual.

A bad complexion?

Harmony or conflict in society were thought to correspond to events written in the skies by the wandering of the planets and in miniature within the individual. The position of the planets and stars at the moment of birth was thought to determine a person's 'temperament': Conrade was **born under Saturn** (*Act 1 Scene 3, lines 8–9*), which supposedly produced a gloomy character; Benedick regrets that he was **not born under a rhyming planet** (*Act 5 Scene 2, line 28*) while the high-spirited Beatrice was born, apparently, under a star that danced (*Act 2 Scene 1, lines 250–1*).

Similarly the natural world was divided into four elements – fire (the most noble), air, water and earth (the lowest) – and resembled the human body which was thought to be made up of four corresponding liquids or humours which were created from food in the liver. The four humours were melancholy (or black bile), phlegm, blood and choler (or yellow bile). Each of these corresponded to the four elements and to the four seasons – autumn, winter, spring and summer. The correspondences may be set out like this:

Element	*Humour*	*Quality*	*Nature*
Fire	Choler (yellow bile)	Hot and dry	Choleric (angry, temperamental)
Air	Blood	Hot and moist	Sanguine (jolly, lusty)
Water	Phlegm	Cold and moist	Phlegmatic (sluggish, slow)
Earth	Melancholy (black bile)	Cold and dry	Melancholic (sad, lovesick)

When Beatrice notices Claudio's jealousy she compares him to a Seville orange because the colour yellow was thought to indicate the yellow bile that produced **that jealous complexion** *(Act 2 Scene 1, line 220)*. Don John's **melancholy disposition** *(Act 2 Scene 1, line 5)* arises from a predominance of 'black bile' in the body whereas Beatrice has **little of the melancholy element in her** *(Act 2 Scene 1, line 255)*.

Ideally the humours were in balance but in practice one would normally dominate, giving the person a particular temperament or 'complexion' (literally, a mixture). Thus 'humour' came to mean a particular type of personality: too much black bile produced depression (i.e. melancholy); too much phlegm made people apathetic (i.e. phlegmatic); too much blood made them cheerful (i.e. sanguine); and too much choler quick-tempered (i.e. choleric). Doctors often 'bled' their patients by drawing blood from an arm or foot to restore balance, because blood was considered to have pre-eminence over the other humours.

The Bastard

Context and Character

The Bastard character – Don John in *Much Ado About Nothing* – was a common figure on the Elizabethan stage. He was nearly always presented in totally negative terms as a malcontent and outsider, a disturber of harmony and at war with himself and with society.

The representation of the bastard as conventional stage villain had strong historical reasons. The very stability of society then depended on the inheritance of land and property. The claims of an illegitimate child could threaten that stability.

In Shakespeare's time the law of *primogeniture* forbade the bastard from inheriting. Even if the bastard was born before his legitimate brother and had been acknowledged, brought up and educated by his father, he still had no claim. It was a custom that inevitably nurtured resentment.

The character Edmund in Shakespeare's play *King Lear* makes a good case for bastards against the unfairness of society which – through no fault of their own – deprived them of many basic rights.

>   Wherefore should I
> Stand in the plague of custom, and permit
> The curiosity of nations to deprive me,
> For that I am some twelve or fourteen moon-shines   5
> Lag of a brother? Why bastard? Wherefore base?
> When my dimensions are as well compact,
> My mind as generous, and my shape as true,
> As honest madam's issue? Why brand they us
> With base? with baseness? bastardy? base, base?   10
> Who, in the lusty stealth of nature, take
> More composition and fierce quality
> Than doth, within a dull, stale, tired bed,
> Go to the creating a whole tribe of fops,
> Got 'tween asleep and wake? Well, then,   15
> Legitimate Edgar, I must have your land:
> Our father's love is to the bastard Edmund
> As to the legitimate: fine word, – 'legitimate'!
> Well, my legitimate, if this letter speed,
> And my invention thrive, Edmund the base   20
> Shall top the legitimate. I grow; I prosper:
> Now, gods, stand up for bastards!
> *(Act 1 Scene 2)*

- Nevertheless, Edmund is portrayed as an unscrupulous and inhumanly cruel villain greedy for his legitimate brother's inheritance. As he says in line 16: **Legitimate Edgar, I must have your land.**

- The subject of bastardy was a particularly sensitive one in Shakespeare's time. Queen Elizabeth was herself regarded as illegitimate by her Catholic enemies. She was the daughter of King Henry VIII and his second wife, Anne Boleyn. Her father had divorced his first wife, Katherine of Aragon, without the Pope's permission and many therefore regarded the second marriage as unlawful.

- Refer to Character Sheets 53 and 54 on Don John for more information about the role of the Bastard in *Much Ado About Nothing*.

Beatrice (1)

**...there was a star danced and under that
I was born** (*Act 2 Scene 1, lines 250–1*)

Act 1 Scene 1

How would you describe Beatrice's skirmish of wit with the Messenger: surprising, inappropriate, aggressive, inventive, subversive, embarrassing, unwomanly...?

_____

_____

_____

Is Beatrice a match for Benedick in their opening **skirmish of wit**? Do you take her criticisms of him seriously – does *she* take them seriously?

_____

_____

_____

Is there evidence in this scene that Beatrice and Benedick might have a romantic history? Look out for evidence in other scenes (NB Act 2 Scene 1, lines 207–10). Could there be any connection between their past and her scorn of love and marriage?

_____

_____

_____

Act 2 Scene 1

What objections to marriage does Beatrice reveal in the opening section (lines 1–60)? How is her own position different from that of Hero, and how are Beatrice and Hero contrasted?

_____

_____

_____

Is there any difference between the private (lines 92–114) and public exchanges of witty banter between Beatrice and Benedick?

_____

_____

_____

Does Beatrice's conversation with Don Pedro (lines 234–51) reveal a different side of her character?

_____

_____

_____

Why is Beatrice sent on an errand (fictitious?) by Leonato (line 252)?

_____

_____

Beatrice (2)

Act 2 Scene 3

What insights does the gulling of Benedick reveal of the character and attitudes of Beatrice?

_____

_____

_____

Benedick is forced to admit that Beatrice has many fine qualities. List them. How close do they come to his earlier model of his 'ideal' woman (see lines 20–7)?

_____

_____

Act 3 Scene 1

What are the criticisms that Hero and the others make of Beatrice? Are they justified?

_____

_____

In the final speech of the scene, does Beatrice's conversion to the idea of marriage owe more to her realisation of Benedick's virtues – or to the criticisms of her own character?

_____

_____

Act 3 Scene 4

Do you see any change in Beatrice now that she has apparently bid farewell to **Contempt** and **maiden pride** *(Act 3 Scene 1, line 109)*? Does she seem to be on the defensive, for once?

_____

_____

Act 4 Scene 1

In the final episode of the scene, how does Beatrice react to Benedick's expressions of love: with enthusiasm, indifference, uncertainty, confusion, anxiety, anger? Explain her reactions.

_____

_____

_____

Do you think that Beatrice manipulates Benedick's feelings in the episode?

_____

_____

_____

Beatrice (3)

Act 4 Scene 1

The word-play between Beatrice and Benedick continues but now the context is deadly serious. Make a note of the ways in which they use ideas of **swearing/ protesting love** and **eating words/swords**.

_____

_____

_____

In what ways do we see a 'new' Beatrice in this scene?

_____

_____

_____

Act 5 Scene 2

Do Beatrice and Benedick move emotionally closer in this scene, do you think? How is this shown? Does Beatrice show more interest in the course of Benedick's love than previously?

_____

_____

_____

How do external events still inhibit them from exploring and expressing their feelings freely?

_____

_____

_____

Act 5 Scene 4

Benedick had said that he and Beatrice were **too wise to woo peaceably** (*Act 5 Scene 2, line 52*) yet in the final scene she is discovered to have written a love sonnet and is finally silenced with a kiss. Has she finally conformed?

_____

_____

_____

Discussion

Do you see Beatrice as an intelligent, imaginative, unconventional feminist, or a bitter and frustrated ageing spinster – or what?

Benedick (1)

...it is certain I am loved of all ladies, only you excepted. *(Act 1 Scene 1, lines 92–3)*

Act 1 Scene 1

Before Benedick arrives on stage we have been given a catalogue of his failings by Beatrice. Make a note of them.

_____

_____

_____

When he arrives, how does he compare with Beatrice's description of him?

_____

_____

_____

Note down the insults that Benedick directs at Beatrice. Are they unkind or good-humoured? What is your impression of their relationship at this stage?

_____

_____

_____

What seem to be Benedick's views of women, love and marriage? Are they presented as being particularly suited to the all-male soldiers' world of Benedick and his comrades-in-arms?

_____

_____

_____

_____

Benedick's wit conjures up fantastic, outlandish word cartoons. He often uses hyperbole (exaggeration) for comic effect. Find some examples and say how they are effective.

_____

_____

_____

In Benedick's conversation with Claudio, do you get the impression that in scorning the idea of love and marriage he is in some ways acting out a role? What gives this impression?

_____

_____

Benedick (2)

Act 2 Scene 1

Beatrice describes Benedick as **the Prince's jester** *(line 103)*. Court jesters were given special permission to mock their 'betters' and set aside the normal rules of good manners and decorum. Is this true of Benedick?

_____

_____

_____

Look at the conversation between Benedick and Claudio (lines 140–54). How, like Claudio, has Benedick misunderstood the present situation?

_____

_____

_____

Benedick is genuinely hurt by Beatrice's criticisms of him. Has his vanity been punctured – or does he really want her to think well of him? Notice that when he is alone he calls her **Lady Beatrice** *(line 156)*; when he speaks publicly she is **Lady Tongue** *(lines 205–6)*.

_____

_____

_____

Benedick seems to try to ensure that no one takes him seriously. However, note his honourable qualities listed by Don Pedro (lines 279–86).

_____

_____

_____

Act 2 Scene 3

Look carefully at Benedick's soliloquy (lines 7–27). What does he most scorn about love – and is he in the right mood to change his mind?

_____

_____

_____

In his next soliloquy (lines 173–90) note down the various stages by which he comes to the conclusion that he will love Beatrice.

_____

_____

_____

Benedick (3)

Act 3 Scene 2

Note down the ways in which, once Benedick has admitted that he has fallen in love, he changes into the conventional lover that he has previously scorned.

_____

_____

_____

Act 4 Scene 1

Notice the ways Benedick refers to **honour** in this scene (e.g. *lines 181 and 242*). How is 'honour' the basis of the choice he ultimately makes between Beatrice and the male military code he had previously shared with Claudio and Don Pedro?

_____

_____

_____

The first meeting between Benedick and Beatrice as lovers is far from conventional. To what extent do they admit their love for each other here and how is it qualified?

_____

_____

_____

_____

Act 5 Scene 1

Claudio and Don Pedro completely misjudge Benedick in this scene. He has changed; they, apparently, have not. In what ways has Benedick grown in moral stature during the episode?

_____

_____

_____

_____

Act 5 Scene 2

The conversation between the lovers is much lighter in tone than their previous meeting. How does their relationship progress in this scene?

_____

_____

_____

Benedick (4)

Act 5 Scene 2

Find examples of a more gentle humour between them compared with the aggressive wit of their former **merry war.**

_____

_____

_____

_____

Act 5 Scene 4

There are still signs of hesitancy and uncertainty in Benedick as he 'takes the plunge' to marry Beatrice. Can you find evidence – and can you explain his hesitancy even at this stage?

_____

_____

_____

How do you think the marriage between Benedick and Beatrice will be different from that of Claudio and Hero? Which is likely to be the more successful?

_____

_____

_____

_____

How does Benedick try to restore his friendship with Don Pedro and Claudio? Does he fully succeed, do you think?

_____

_____

_____

Benedick speaks the final words of the play. Is that significant, do you think? Look at what he says and how he says it.

_____

_____

_____

Discussion

'Beginning the play as a self-regarding and insecure male chauvinist Benedick develops both dignity and maturity without losing his sense of the ridiculous.' How much truth is there in this claim?

Leonato (1)

Bring me a father that so loved his child...
(Act 5 Scene 1, line 8)

Act 1 Scene 1

Leonato supplies the audience with several pieces of important information in this scene. List them briefly (with line references).

_____

_____

_____

Leonato's manner can be over-formal. Find examples of his exaggerated formality. Look for instances of patterned language.

_____

_____

Act 1 Scene 2

How does Leonato react to the (mistaken) news that Don Pedro intends to propose marriage to his daughter, Hero?

_____

_____

Act 2 Scene 1

Leonato joins in bawdy repartee with Beatrice. Find examples. How does this affect your view of him? What about his daughter's feelings?

_____

_____

_____

How does Leonato react when he realises that it is Claudio who wants to marry Hero and not the Prince? Does he object? Why, do you think?

_____

_____

Look at the things Leonato says to and about Beatrice in this scene. She is his niece and he is her guardian (see Act 2 Scene 3, line 136) but does he find her something of an embarrassment? Does he treat her differently from his daughter, Hero?

_____

_____

Act 2 Scene 3

What contribution does Leonato make to the gulling of Benedick? Is he always as quick-witted as Don Pedro and Claudio?

_____

_____

Leonato (2)

Act 3 Scene 2

Does Leonato join in the teasing of Benedick as much as the two younger men?

_____

_____

Act 3 Scene 5

How far can Leonato's role in the play be seen as **the white-bearded fellow**
(Act 2 Scene 3, line 102), an authority figure behaving sensibly and responsibly?
How does he deal with Dogberry and Verges?

_____

_____

_____

Act 4 Scene 1

Look carefully at Leonato's role in the first part of the scene, until Hero faints and her
accusers leave (line 107). At what points is he: impatient; cheerful and confident;
puzzled; anxious but broad-minded; bewildered; severe; selfish? Quote and explain.

_____

_____

_____

What are Leonato's feelings as he rebukes Hero when she revives from her faint?
Can you explain the violence of his reaction? Do you have any sympathy for him
at any point during the rest of the scene?

_____

_____

_____

Act 5 Scene 1

Leonato appears inconsolable in his grief (lines 3–38). How does he explain the
intensity of his feelings? Do you sympathise with him or is his grief self-indulgent?

_____

_____

_____

Leonato has previously spoken of taking revenge (Act 4 Scene 1, lines 186–95).
Now he tries to challenge Claudio to a duel. Is he concerned primarily with
Hero's reputation, or his own?

_____

_____

_____

Leonato (3)

Act 5 Scene 1

Do you find Leonato's confrontation with Claudio and the Prince dignified and moving, or ridiculous? Find evidence.

_____

_____

_____

_____

When Borachio's deceit is uncovered later in the scene, Leonato performs both private and public roles as injured father and conscientious magistrate. What qualities does he reveal in this episode? Does your attitude towards him change?

_____

_____

_____

_____

Act 5 Scene 4

What is Leonato's role in the final scene: director, or supporting actor – or both?

_____

_____

_____

_____

Discussion

'The picture of old age in the play is unflattering – conventional, hypocritical, rash and morally blind. The old are responsible for the world which youth has to strive against and try to remake.' Is this the best that can be said of Leonato?

Claudio (1)

In mine eye she is the sweetest lady that ever I looked on. *(Act 1 Scene 1, line138)*

Act 1 Scene 1

By the time Claudio arrives on stage we have already been given important information about him. What impression have you formed of him?

_____

_____

_____

When Claudio arrives with Don Pedro and his companions he says nothing until he is alone with Benedick. Why, do you think?

_____

_____

What are the qualities that cause him to fall in love with Hero? Is he idealistic? Are all of his motives noble?

_____

_____

_____

How is Claudio's idea of love and marriage contrasted with that of Benedick in this scene? Do you think either of them is correct in his view?

_____

_____

_____

Act 2 Scene 1

How does Claudio react to Don John's deceitful distortion of Don Pedro's wooing of Hero? Whom does he blame for this 'betrayal'?

_____

_____

_____

Claudio is eager to join in a trick to 'deceive' Benedick on the subject of love. Is this surprising when he himself has just been deceived about love by Don John?

_____

_____

_____

Act 2 Scene 3

What is Claudio's contribution to the gulling of Benedick? How does he 'use' Hero during this episode?

_____

_____

_____

Claudio (2)

Act 3 Scene 2

Do you find Claudio's teasing of Benedick good-humoured or crude and excessive? Is he paying Benedick back for mocking his own love for Hero in Act 1 Scene 1?

_____

_____

How does Claudio react to Don John's claims about Hero's being **disloyal** *(line 74)*? Is he too ready to believe her guilty? Is he concerned about her 'honour' – or his own?

_____

_____

Act 4 Scene 1

Does Claudio have your sympathy when he dramatically seizes control of the marriage ceremony? To what extent was his intervention 'staged'?

_____

Is Claudio needlessly cruel, high-minded, sincere, irrational, arrogant, self-righteous…?

_____

_____

Make a note of the emotive language – negative and positive – that Claudio uses to refer to Hero. What conclusions can you draw? Has Claudio's love for Hero ever been very mature?

_____

_____

_____

Act 5 Scene 1

Does Claudio gain your respect in the dialogue with Leonato and Antonio? How would you describe his manner?

_____

_____

Claudio has just been told that Hero is dead. How would you describe his response when Benedick enters (line 109–10): callous, flippant, in need of diversion, insensitive, inconsiderate, witty, courageous…?

_____

Claudio (3)

Act 5 Scene 1

When Claudio learns from Borachio the truth of the plot to shame Hero, does his regret seem genuine? How?

_____

_____

_____

Act 5 Scene 3

Some have seen Claudio's ritual of penance as an enforced token gesture lacking any real remorse; others see it as revealing a 'new', chastened and more mature Claudio. What do you think?

_____

_____

_____

_____

Act 5 Scene 4

Look at Claudio's speeches prior to the unmasking of Hero (lines 38–72). Does he seem to have changed significantly? Is he, after all, a very likeable young man?

_____

_____

How does he react when Hero is unmasked? Is his gratitude genuine?

_____

_____

_____

Discussion

'Claudio is a dreamer who requires a wife of beauty, wealth and status to match his vision of his own nobility.' Is this being too hard on Claudio?

Hero (1)

Oh God defend me, how am I beset!

(Act 4 Scene 1, line 72)

Act 1 Scene 1

Hero is referred to (lines 76–85) and then Claudio speaks of his love for her. List her qualities as described (with references).

_____

_____

_____

Hero says nothing in this scene. Why? How does her silence affect your opinion of her – and her relationship with others?

_____

_____

_____

Act 1 Scene 2

Again Hero is spoken of. What does this brief reference add to your understanding?

_____

_____

_____

Act 1 Scene 3

Yet again Hero is the subject of others' speculation. What other perspective does this offer of Hero? Does it conflict with early impressions of her?

_____

_____

_____

Act 2 Scene 1

Hero speaks for the first time (line 5). About whom? How have Hero and Don John paralleled each other so far in the play?

_____

_____

Does Hero's conversation with Don Pedro (lines 61–71) reveal a different side of her? Does the masquerade and Don Pedro's disguise give her more freedom to express herself?

_____

_____

How does Hero behave when Don Pedro announces that he has successfully wooed her for Claudio (lines 223–37)? Is this consistent with her earlier behaviour?

_____

_____

Hero (2)

Act 2 Scene 1

How does Hero react to Don Pedro's plan to trick Benedick and Beatrice into marriage (lines 277–8)? Is she enthusiastic?

_____

_____

_____

Act 3 Scene 1

Hero seems more playful and less inhibited during the gulling of Beatrice. Why, do you think? Is her own role different in this scene from that in her previous appearances?

_____

_____

_____

Are you totally convinced by this 'new' Hero? Does she give an entirely convincing 'performance' for the hidden Beatrice?

_____

_____

_____

What do Hero's observations about Beatrice tell you about the way she sees her own role in respect of marriage and that of women in general?

_____

_____

_____

Act 3 Scene 4

How does Hero respond to the banter about dresses and husbands in this scene?

_____

_____

_____

Does the audience's knowledge of the progress of Don John's plot affect the way we respond to Hero here?

_____

_____

_____

Act 4 Scene 1

Hero is the focal point of this dramatic scene but her own spoken contribution to it is very limited. Make a note of the various views of Hero that emerge from the words of others. How do you react to them?

_____

_____

_____

Hero (3)

Act 4 Scene 1

Look at Hero's only substantial speech in the scene (lines 172–9). What does it reveal of her response to her society's attitude towards female honour?

_____

_____

_____

Although Hero says little, ironically her fainting makes possible the Friar's plan to restore Claudio to her. Does anyone ask her opinion of the Friar's scheme?

_____

_____

_____

Act 5 Scene 4

Look at Hero's language after the unmasking. Note the link between reputation, dishonour and death.

_____

_____

_____

Discussion

'The character of Hero is merely an emblem or symbol to allow other people to strike attitudes.' What do you think?

Don Pedro (1)

...the time shall not go dully by us.
(Act 2 Scene 1, line 269)

Act 1 Scene 1

Don Pedro, Prince of Arragon, is the highest-ranking of Messina's aristocrats. How is this shown in the opening scene? How do others behave towards him?

_____

_____

_____

Claudio is in love; Benedick scorns love. Where does Don Pedro stand on the subject and what do you learn of his character and attitudes from the advice he gives to Claudio?

_____

_____

_____

Act 2 Scene 1

Do his wooing and bestowing of Hero reveal other aspects of his personality?

_____

_____

_____

Don Pedro offers marriage to Beatrice. It is also Don Pedro who devises the plan to trick Beatrice and Benedick into marriage. What do you judge to be his motives?

_____

_____

_____

Act 2 Scene 3

Note down the contribution that Don Pedro makes to the gulling of Benedick. In what ways does he direct the episode?

_____

_____

_____

Act 3 Scene 2

How does Don Pedro contribute to the teasing of Benedick? Does he tend to initiate ideas while others back him up with supporting comments?

_____

_____

_____

Is Don Pedro too quick to believe his brother's accusations against Hero? How does he respond now that Don John has seized the initiative?

_____

_____

_____

Don Pedro (2)

Act 4 Scene 1

Can you find evidence of collusion between Claudio and Don Pedro to shame Hero in the most humiliating way? How does this affect your view of him?

_____

_____

_____

Act 5 Scene 1

Note down instances of Don Pedro's behaviour towards Leonato and Antonio and of his response to the report of Hero's 'death'. How would you judge his behaviour?

_____

_____

_____

How do you judge his attempts at light-hearted banter with Benedick: witty, callous, insensitive, strained, ill-judged, well-intentioned?

_____

_____

_____

How far does he redeem himself in his reactions to Borachio's confession?

_____

_____

_____

Act 5 Scene 3

How does Don Pedro introduce an important symbolic change of tone in this solemn scene?

_____

_____

_____

Act 5 Scene 4

At the end of the play Benedick observes: **Prince. Thou art sad ...** *(line 115)*. Why, do you think?

_____

_____

Discussion

'A frivolous and shallow character whose narrow sense of honour and of his own importance are emotionally crippling.' Is there any truth in this judgement of Don Pedro?

Don John (1)

> I had rather be a canker in a hedge than a rose in his grace. *(Act 1 Scene 3, line 19)*

Act 1 Scene 1
How do Don John's very few words in this scene (see line 116) immediately set him apart from the other characters and change the mood of the scene?

_____

_____

Act 1 Scene 3
What do lines 1–28 tell us about (a) Don John's attitudes, (b) his motives and (c) his relationship with his brother, Don Pedro?

_____

_____

_____

How do Don John's speech patterns reflect his character in these lines?

_____

_____

_____

Does his reaction to Borachio's news confirm your first impressions of him? What is Don John's particular grievance against Claudio?

_____

_____

_____

Act 2 Scene 1
Is the comparison between Don John and Benedick (see lines 1–13) a helpful one? Do the two men seem to share a particular view of marriage?

_____

_____

_____

How does Don John first try to make trouble between his brother and Claudio (see lines 115–28) – and how far is he successful on this occasion?

_____

_____

_____

Act 2 Scene 2
How is Don John dependent on his henchmen – particularly Borachio – for his ideas? Does this make him less base – or more so?

_____

_____

Make a note of the language in this scene that has to do with ideas of wickedness, disease and death. How does the language contribute to your perception of Don John?

_____

_____

Don John (2)

Act 3 Scene 2

Don John always expects the worst of others and exploits their vulnerabilities for his own perverse satisfaction. What weaknesses does he hope to exploit in the plan to deceive Claudio?

_____

_____

_____

Look at the way Don John tells Claudio and Don Pedro about Hero's 'dishonesty' (lines 57–98). How does he manipulate their feelings?

_____

_____

_____

Act 4 Scene 1

Usually Don John perpetrates his mischief by taking people aside and speaking to them privately. This is the only scene in which he shows his hand in public. How does he contribute to the denunciation of Hero?

_____

_____

_____

Act 5 Scene 1

When Borachio confesses his part in the plot to dishonour Hero (lines 199–209) is he entirely honest about Don John's part in it?

_____

_____

_____

How do Borachio's confession and apparent repentance affect the audience's view of Don John?

_____

_____

_____

Act 5 Scene 4

How does news of Don John's capture affect the mood at the end of the play?

_____

_____

Discussion

'Don John and Hero are opposed throughout the play but they are both victims in a society bound by restrictive conventions'. Do you agree?

GCSE Coursework Assignment

In *Much Ado About Nothing* characters are often mistaken by appearances. Show how Shakespeare uses these mistakes for comedy and for dramatic effect.

I have deceived even your very eyes

(Act 5 Scene 1, line 200)

Write about these points:

- When and why characters are deliberately misled.
- How characters can sometimes be deceived for good motives.
- The ways that characters deceive or 'practise' on others for malicious reasons.
- The ways that we as audience react to the mistakes that we see taking place on stage: when do we enjoy them and when are we shocked?

A suitable plan for the coursework assignment could be as follows.

1 To show how both Beatrice and Benedick display their dislike of each other and their opposition to marriage in general.
2 To explain how Beatrice and Benedick are tricked into falling in love with each other.
3 To discuss the character of Don John and his jealousy of Claudio.
4 To explain the two plots in which he deceives Claudio.
5 To show how far – and why – each plot is successful and the effect the plots have on others.
6 To explain how tragedy is avoided and harmony restored.
7 To explore how the audience enjoys being in on the trick played on Beatrice and Benedick but dismayed when Don John's deception threatens disaster.

Explain your ideas and support them with quotations.

Assignment guidance

Act 1

- Examine Benedick's and Beatrice's attitudes to each other and to marriage.
- Look at how their attitudes to love contrast with Claudio's.
- Look at the ways in which Don John's character and motives are established.
- Examine his first attempt to cause trouble.

Act 2

- The masked ball provides the perfect setting for confused identities, deliberate deception and mistaken points of view.
- Don John deceives Claudio about Don Pedro's motives. How far is his plan successful?
- Do you think the audience is meant to take Beatrice and Benedick's 'merry war' seriously – or do they deceive themselves about their real feelings?

- Don Pedro outlines his plan to trick Benedick and Beatrice into falling in love.
- Borachio and Don John devise a plot to shame Hero. Explore the main differences between this plot and Don Pedro's trick.
- The tricking of Benedick includes many 'home truths'. Look at Benedick's reactions.

Act 3

- Like Benedick, Beatrice learns painful truths from her deceivers – but does she take much convincing?
- Benedick eagerly adopts the **old signs** *(Scene 2, lines 30–1)* of the conventional lover. How does the audience react?
- Claudio is led to believe that he can trust the evidence of his eyes – but can he?
- Notice that it is a wonderful comic irony that the foolish Watch come to know and understand the truth better than their so-called 'betters'.

Act 4

Show how the 'seeming' shame of Hero is exposed while her real innocence remains hidden.

- The Friar offers some hope – ironically his plan is based on yet another deception.
- Explain how Beatrice and Benedick's first meeting as 'lovers' is affected by earlier events.
- Show how dramatic tension is created by Dogberry's incompetence.

Act 5

- Show how the false shaming of Hero affects the friendship of Benedick and his former comrades.
- Explain how tragedy is narrowly avoided and Hero's innocence acknowledged.
- Look at how the final deception played on Claudio reveals a 'new' Hero and makes possible a joyful double marriage.

Activities Sheet	Title	Act/Scene
4	Don John	Act 1 Scene 3
7	Something and not[h]ing	Act 1 Scene 1
8	'Know me and not know me...'	Act 2 Scene 1
9	'...seeming truth...'	Act 2 Scene 2
11	'...some with traps'	Act 3 Scene 1
17	Plots in parallel	Act 4 Scene 1
18	The happiest day...?	Act 4 Scene 1
19	A woman's role	Act 4 Scene 1
21	Age before duty?	Act 5 Scene 1
22	'Too wise to woo peaceably...'	Act 5 Scene 2
24	'And all lived happily...'?	Act 5 Scene 4

GCSE Coursework Assignment

'Much Ado About Nothing is a richly comic play.'
- **Examine some of the ways in which comedy is created.**
- **How can the different sorts of comedy be conveyed to an audience?**

Types of comedy to look for:
- Comedy through language:
  a) language used wittily or inventively (e.g. puns, hyperbole) on a variety of subjects: love and sexuality; classical legend and mythology; war and chivalry
  b) unconscious misuse of language.

- Comedy through characterisation:
  a) the 'merry war'
  b) Dogberry's self-importance; the comic rivalry between Dogberry and Verges
  c) contrast in attitudes – between Benedick and Claudio on love.

- Comedy of situation:
  a) the tricking of Benedick and Beatrice
  b) the questioning of prisoners by Dogberry.

  This sort of comedy is improved when the audience is 'in' on the joke and knows more than some of the characters or when there is ironic or comic contrast.

- Visual comedy:
  a) comic business
  b) costumes and props.

Assignment guidance

You will be able to make use of some of the following points. Develop the most appropriate material with your own comments and supporting detail.

Act 1
- Beatrice and Benedick exchange witty insults for their own satisfaction and for public entertainment.
- Benedick mocks Claudio on the subject of love – his use of hyperbole (exaggeration) suggests his attitude is partly a pose.

Act 2
- The masked ball with its opportunities for fantastical costume, music and light-hearted atmosphere has plenty of potential for comic business.
- Beatrice wickedly exploits Benedick's belief that she doesn't recognise him.
- Benedick relishes gloating 'I told you so' when Claudio believes he has been deceived in love by Don Pedro.
- Benedick takes his revenge on Beatrice in a series of comic verbal cartoon images (see Scene 1, lines 180–206).

- The passionate opposition of Beatrice and Benedick to the idea of love and marriage makes them the perfect subjects for a comic 'sting'.
- There is plenty of scope for comic business as Don Pedro, Claudio and Leonato improvise a conversation to entrap Benedick.
- Benedick's out-of-character reactions to what he hears present plenty of opportunities for comedy.

Act 3

- Plenty of scope for comic business as Beatrice hides and listens – and in her reactions to the harsh things being said about her. Her 'conversion' to love is just as abrupt as Benedick's.
- Benedick's changed appearance to match his new role as 'lover' – there is plenty of comic mileage in his friends' reactions and his embarrassment.
- The Watch: opportunities for unsuitable costumes, improvised prop-weapons and slap-stick business – inept drilling?
- Dogberry's seriousness and pride are in comic contrast to his incompetence and constant misuse of language.
- The detention of Borachio (drunk) and Conrade by the Watch provides the opportunity for comic business.
- Comic rivalry between Dogberry and Verges as they report to Leonato the detention of two **arrant knaves** (*Scene 5, line 25*).

Act 4

- Dogberry relishes his moment of glory in directing the examination of Borachio and Conrade – his ignorance of proper procedures and his insistence on trivialities is richly comic.

Act 5

- Don Pedro and Claudio's attempts to draw Benedick into witty banter now seem callous and ill-timed.
- Dogberry's delivery of his prisoners momentarily lightens the profoundly serious mood as the truth emerges.
- As the plot's complications begin to unravel, Benedick's flawed attempts at playing the lover lighten the atmosphere, as does a resumption of the witty sparring between the lovers.
- Benedick and Beatrice are still reluctant to admit their love in public but are trapped by the evidence of their respective love sonnets.

Activities Sheet	Title	Act/Scene
1	Round one…!	Act 1 Scene 1
2	Comrades-in-arms	Act 1 Scene 1
6	Styles and titles	Act 1 Scene 1
8	'Know me and not know me…'	Act 2 Scene 1
10	Benedick and the 'love-gods'	Act 2 Scene 3
11	'…some with traps'	Act 3 Scene 1
12	Symptoms of love	Act 3 Scene 2
13	Law and order	Act 3 Scene 3
14	*Mal à propos*	Act 3 Scene 3
16	'…great haste' – less speed	Act 3 Sscene 5
20	The examination	Act 4 Scene 2
22	'Too wise to woo peaceably…'	Act 5 Scene 2

GCSE Coursework Assignment

The play has something for everybody in the audience – comedy, romance and villainy. Write about two or three scenes in which Shakespeare has used those ingredients to appeal to a wide audience.

Some issues to consider:

- The illegitimate Don John embodies the villainous aspects of the play.
- Note down deliberate acts of vindictive wickedness. Do the victims contribute to their own downfall?
- Notice that appearances can be deceptive. Why can't some characters distinguish between real virtue and 'seeming' virtue, real truth and 'seeming' truth?
- The language of war permeates the play – look, too, for images of violence, death, torture and disease.
- The 'sufferings' of love are repeatedly referred to – are they just a courtly convention or are they real?
- Notice how 'love' is influenced by money and property.
- Is Benedick's friendship with Don Pedro and Claudio always constructive and benign?
- Is the so-called 'merry war' between Beatrice and Benedick always good-natured – or is it sometimes malicious?
- Could the staging of the 'darker' scenes contribute to their effect: costume, lighting, sound?

A possible essay plan might be:

1 Establish that even the comic aspects of the play have a darker undercurrent: background of war, jokes can be personal and hurtful, language draws on images of violence, torture.
2 Discuss the presentation of Don John's character, his illegitimacy and his jealousy of his brother and Claudio.
3 Outline the two malicious schemes against Claudio and Hero.
4 Examine the contribution to the success of his plots of weakness in others: jealousy, lack of trust, false ideas of 'love' and 'honour'.
5 Show that the darker aspects of the play are counterbalanced by comic equivalents: tricks and deception; personal weakness/vulnerability; attitudes to love.
6 Show how the villainous and comic strands of the play combine and crises are resolved to produce a harmonious conclusion.

Assignment guidance

Act 1

- Notice that the play begins against the background of an internal dynastic war caused by jealousy and a sense of injustice.
- There are several early references to killing – are they completely cancelled out by the humorous context?
- Don John is a self-confessed malcontent. Has his illegitimacy caused his resentment – or is he naturally 'bad'?

Act 2

- Don John's attempt to sour the wooing of Hero is partly successful. What does this reveal about Claudio?
- Look at Claudio's idea of the relationship between 'love' and 'friendship'.
- The comic gullings of both Benedick (Act 2 Scene 3) and Beatrice (Act 3 Scene 1) contain some painful 'home truths'.

Act 3

- Why are Claudio and Don Pedro so ready to believe in the guilt of Hero? What does this reveal about their attitude to women and their own idea of 'honour'?
- The scene that they 'witness' is represented in the text only by Borachio's report of it. Could 'staging' the scene affect your attitude?

Act 4

- The manner in which Hero is denounced is deliberately cruel and humiliating. How does this affect your view of Claudio and Don Pedro?
- Look at the ways in which Hero is abandoned by both Claudio and her father, from whom she might have expected loyalty. What is the effect of this?
- Look at the language used to speak of 'innocence' and 'shame'.
- Hero will need to **die to live** *(Scene 1, line 248)*. Is the Friar's plan cruel or can it be justified?
- Benedick is forced to prove his love for Beatrice by undertaking to **Kill Claudio** *(Scene 1, line 277)* – an important choice between 'love' and 'friendship'.

Act 5

- What methods are Leonato and Antonio prepared to employ to avenge themselves on Claudio and Don Pedro (see also Act 4 Scene 1, lines 185–95)? Can they be justified?
- How do Claudio and Don Pedro behave towards Leonato and Antonio?
- What is the effect of Claudio's solemn ritual of penance (Scene 3)? Again staging will establish its tone.
- Is Benedick's friendship with Claudio and Don Pedro fully restored at the end of the play?
- The report of Don John's capture in the final moments brings a sombre note to the wedding celebrations.

Activities Sheet	Title	Act/Scene
1	Round one…!	Act 1 Scene 1
4	Don John	Act 1 Scene 3
5	Men's talk	Act 1 Scene 1
7	Something and not[h]ing	Act 1 Scene 1
8	'Know me and not know me…'	Act 2 Scene 1
9	'…seeming truth…'	Act 2 Scene 2
13	Law and order	Act 3 Scene 3
17	Plots in parallel	Act 4 Scene 1
18	The happiest day…?	Act 4 Scene 1
19	A woman's role	Act 4 Scene 1
21	Age before duty?	Act 5 Scene 1
24	'And all lived happily…'?	Act 5 Scene 4

GCSE Coursework Assignment

Friendship is constant in all things,
Save in the office and affairs of love.
(Act 2 Scene 1, lines 132–3)

In this assignment you are asked to think about friendship as it is presented in the play and to give an oral presentation in which you discuss (a) the way characters behave and react in the play and (b) what you think about attitudes to friendship today.

For a modern reader and theatre audience a play by Shakespeare is always a strange mixture of the familiar and unfamiliar.

- The stories are about people who are in many ways just like us: young people form friendships, fall out with each other, fall in – and out of – love, get jealous, enjoy practical jokes; they can be funny, spiteful, supportive, loyal, selfish, shallow, insecure and foolish.

- However, you might find some of their attitudes to the opposite sex, authority, chastity and marriage, honour, reputation and revenge to be very different from your own.

This is an assignment that could work in groups of three members of the same sex or possibly in groups of four with two males and two females who might represent different viewpoints.

Try to put together a presentation which has range and variety: singly/in pairs/whole group; play-based attitudes/modern-day points of view.

Your presentation will need to be prepared – but not scripted – and could take place at two or three different times. You could pick-and-mix from the following suggestions or add others of your own.

The play

1 You might like to begin with the whole group discussing the two friendship groups in the play: male (Don Pedro, Claudio, Benedick) and female (Hero, Beatrice, Ursula, Margaret).

Here are some issues you might like to consider:

- What do the two groups have in common and how are they different?

- Does the male group seem to have a stronger bond – is the female friendship more 'loose'? Why?

- What might affect the strength of the bond: age, sex, background, experience, personalities?

- How – and why – do the friendship groups change during the play? Are the characters themselves changed by the events of the play?

2 You could solo role-play one of the characters at a particular point in the play and give a spoken 'diary' in which you talk about your own feelings and thoughts about how your friends have behaved: e.g. Hero the night before she 'marries' Claudio for the second time in the final scene; Claudio following his betrothal to Hero at the masked

party or after being challenged to a duel by Benedick; Benedick after the gulling scene and before he meets his friends in his new role of 'lover'.

You might find it easier to present this as a one-way telephone/mobile conversation with an unseen friend.

Today

3   A modern TV presenter interviews one or more characters from the play for daytime television. He/she will want to challenge some of their actions and attitudes and those of their friends.

4   Imagine that you and a partner might have been members of one of the friendship groups in the play.

   Discuss with your partner how you think you would have fitted in. Do you think you would have got on with all of the other members of the group? What appeals to you – or irritates you – about their personalities? Would you have agreed with their opinions, attitudes and behaviour?

5   As a group discuss the factors that make and break friendships today. You might like to consider some of the following points:

   • What brings about friendship groups: similarities/differences in age, personality, interests? Do you have one main friendship group, two – or more: at school, home, outside team or club?

   • In the play, friends talk largely about relationships, marriage and sex, and they enjoy making jokes at their friends' expense. Is it any different today?

   • What are the main advantages of friendship groups? Are there any drawbacks?

   • Are there any differences between male and female groups? Are they interested in different things? Do they talk and behave differently?

   • In the quotation at the beginning of this assignment, Claudio says that love is the thing that breaks up friendships and the play shows how misunderstanding can threaten to break up friendships. In your experience, what are the things that cause disagreement between friends?

Activities Sheet	Title	Act/Scene
2	Comrades-in-arms	Act 1 Scene 1
5	Men's talk	Act 1 Scene 1
10	Benedick and the 'love-gods'	Act 2 Scene 3
11	'…some with traps'	Act 3 Scene 1
12	Symptoms of love	Act 3 Scene 2
24	'And all lived happily…'?	Act 5 Scene 4

AS Coursework Assignment

5

How far is the title of the play a description of it as a comedy, and how far is it a description of it as a serious message about human follies and frailties?

> **It is not so, nor 'twas not so; but indeed, God forbid it should be so.** *(Act 1 Scene 1, lines 159–60)*

Some issues to consider:

- On the face of it *Much Ado About Nothing* is a flippant, throw-away title such as *As You Like It* and *Twelfth Night: or, What You Will*, which suggests some light and ephemeral diversion. Is the play merely that?

- In Elizabethan speech 'nothing' and 'noting' sounded much the same.

  The play's plot depends on 'noting' – watching, observing, over-hearing – together with reporting and concluding.

  What is the audience's role? We spy on everything!

- The phrase 'much ado' was used to mean a lot of difficulty or bother; it could also mean a lot of action in general. Certainly 'much ado' arises from mistaken or misdirected 'noting' – both comic and potentially tragic.

- The extensive bawdy exchanges of wit in the play invite an implicit pun on the sexual organs. One of the many euphemisms for the male penis is a 'thing' – the woman, of course, having 'no-thing'.

- Some critics believe that the 'nothing' in the title might be an 'in' joke referring to the theatre itself and the opposition which its popularity provoked from the authorities: in 1597, for example, a petition by the Lord Mayor and Aldermen of London stated: 'Firstly, they corrupt youth, containing **nothing** but unchaste matters and ungodly practices…'. Is this too speculative?

  'Nothing' occurs 21 times in the play (including the title); 'noting' = 2; 'note(s)' = 10.

Assignment guidance

Act 1

- Off-stage before the action of the play begins there has been 'much ado' in the campaign against Don John's rebellion – though nothing seems to have changed politically as a result.

- The opening speeches are 'reporting' off-stage action.

- Beatrice and Benedick continue their **skirmish of wit** *(Scene 1, lines 46–7)* – does it amount to anything? Is it merely entertainment for the court or does it express important personal and social issues?

- Claudio has 'noted' Hero – Benedick **noted her not** *(Scene 1, line 120)*. Is love a matter of 'seeing', of personal perspective? Claudio had previously **looked upon her** (Hero) merely with **a soldier's eye** *(Scene 1, line 219)*.

- There is much sexual banter between Benedick and his companions. Are the rituals of the courtly lover (e.g. Claudio) a polite mask for sexual passion ('thing' and 'no-thing') and financial advantage?

- The first 'practice' of the play – Don Pedro will woo Hero in disguise. Don Pedro's 'practice' is overheard, misheard and misreported to Leonato.
- Borachio, too, has overheard the Prince's plan. Ironically his correct hearing will be maliciously misreported.

Act 2

- The masked ball provides several examples of light-hearted disguise, sexual innuendo, misrepresentation and misunderstanding.
- Claudio is misled by Don John; Benedick considers himself **misused** (*Scene 1, line 180*) by Beatrice.
- The **seeming truth of Hero's disloyalty** (*Scene 2, lines 33–4*) will depend on misinterpreting visual evidence
- The 'practice' on Benedick and Beatrice will depend on extended and elaborate instances of 'noting'. Here false evidence will expose the 'true' love between them – and the audience, of course, is always an additional observer.

Act 3

- Beatrice, too, had been unable (or unwilling) to acknowledge Benedick's potential as a husband. Only when **others say thou dost deserve** does she recognise that is **better than reportingly** (*Scene 1, line 116*).
- Don John's 'practice' to shame Hero will involve not only 'evidence' but also reliable witnesses. Claudio is urged to 'trust' the apparently unimpeachable evidence of his own eyes.
- The Watch's 'noting' of Borachio and Conrade brings some hope that Don John's practice will ultimately be thwarted.

Act 4

- All circumstantial evidence – even her blushes – points towards Hero's guilt in the eyes of those conditioned to misinterpret it. Even her father is at first all too ready to believe the reports of his 'betters'.
- Only the impartial Friar **By noting of the lady...** (*Scene 1, line 153*) offers a way out – of course, it will require a further 'practice'.
- The dialogue between Beatrice and Benedick raises many of the unresolved paradoxes of the play: seeming/truth; honour/dishonour; oaths/lies. They coalesce in the 'nothing'/'thing' exchange (Scene 1, lines 260–3).

Act 5

- There are further repercussions of false 'noting' as Claudio and Don Pedro are challenged by Leonato and Antonio and accused of slander and dissembling; they maintain that Hero **was charged with nothing/But what was true, and very full of proof** (*Scene 1, lines 104–5*).
- The 'much ado' arising from 'noting' extends to Benedick's mortally serious challenge to Claudio.
- The true name of Hero is formally and ritually restored with the ritual at her 'tomb'.
- All witness the final 'practice' which reunites Hero and Claudio; Beatrice and Benedick finally realise how they have been 'practised' upon and succumb to the inevitable.

Activities Sheet	Title	Act/Scene
1	Round one…!	Act 1 Scene 1
2	Comrades-in-arms	Act 1 Scene 1
5	Men's talk	Act 1 Scene 1
7	Something and not[h]ing	Act 1 Scene 1
10	Benedick and the 'love-gods'	Act 2 Scene 3
11	'…some with traps'	Act 3 Scene1
14	*Mal à propos*	Act 3 Scene 3
16	'…great haste' – less speed	Act 3 Scene 5
17	Plots in parallel	Act 4 Scene 1
18	The happiest day…?	Act 4 Scene 1
19	A woman's role	Act 4 Scene 1
21	Age before duty?	Act 5 Scene 1
22	'Too wise to woo peaceably…'	Act 5 Scene 2

AS Coursework Assignment

6

How important is the idea of 'honour' in *Much Ado About Nothing*?

...it would better fit your honour to change your mind.
(Act 3 Scene 2, lines 82–3)

Some issues to consider:

- Is honour a very 'fashionable' word today? In what circumstances would you use it?
- Can you think of equivalent modern words that you might use instead?
- Is it a term associated today with particular cultures?
- What do you understand by the word 'honour'?
- Does it seem to have different meanings within the play?
- What does it mean for a man?
- Does it have a different meaning for a woman?
- How far is it connected with moral worth?
- How far is it linked to status and rank?
- To what extent can it be equated with 'reputation'?

Notice the importance of swearing and oath-taking.

Notice the number of times the following words are used in the play. It will help your understanding of the question if you find them and see when, by whom and how they are used:

honour	10	*worthy*	6
honourable	6	*worth*	4
honest	14	*value*	1
dishonour	1		

Are there any other words that might provide additional insights?

Assignment guidance

Act 1

- Honour linked to courage and success in battle – are these values challenged or mocked?
- Are the military values out of place in a 'civilian' context?
- Is Hero presented as an emblem of honour? Look up the story of the Greek legend of Hero and Leander – is this a useful comparison?
- How is Benedick's aversion to marriage linked to his fear of being 'dishonoured'?

Act 2

- Look at Don Pedro's wooing of Hero for Claudio – does this demonstrate the fragility of the idea of reputation as honour?
- Don John suggests that his brother, Don Pedro, has lost honour through his part in the betrothal of Claudio and Hero – how?

Act 3

- Notice how the issue of honour arises even during the gulling of Benedick and Beatrice.

Act 4

- Explore the ways in which the disgracing of Hero raises questions about real and 'seeming' honour.
- Beatrice focuses on the essentially masculine notion of honour killing which becomes a defining issue in the relationship between Beatrice and Benedick.

Act 5

- Leonato and Antonio continue the idea of revenge as a legitimate response against those responsible for dishonouring Hero's reputation.
- Benedick's challenge to Claudio.
- Does Borachio's confession contribute to the restoration of moral order?
- Claudio and Don Pedro are described as **honourable men** (*Scene 1, line 229*). Does Claudio's submission to Leonato's demands restore his honour?

You will find it helpful to read the following Introductory essays in the students' text:

1 Women in a man's world

2 Wooing and wiving

4 Valour, honour and the *duello*

Activities Sheet	Title	Act/Scene
2	Comrades-in-arms	Act 1 Scene 1
4	Don John	Act 1 Scene 3
5	Men's talk	Act 1 Scene 1
6	Styles and titles	Act 1 Scene 1
9	'…seeming truth…'	Act 2 Scene 2
10	Benedick and the 'love-gods'	Act 2 Scene 3
11	'…some with traps'	Act 3 Scene 1
12	Symptoms of love	Act 3 Scene 2
18	The happiest day…?	Act 4 Scene 1
19	A woman's role	Act 4 Scene 1
21	Age before duty?	Act 5 Scene 1
23	Dear Director	Act 5 Scene 3